INTERNATIONAL
RIDING

ERNATIONAL RIDING

ELIZABETH JOHNSON

Contents What's it all about?/9 A history of riding/18
International scene/27 Where do I start?/42
Learning to ride/50 Opportunities to ride/64
International organisations/82 Glossary and further
reading/89 Index/92

THOMAS Y. CROWELL COMPANY
New York/ Established 1834

Acknowledgements

Barnaby's 14, 15, 17 colour; Camera Press 8,
12, 13, 16, 24, 30, 38, 41, 55, 57t, 59, 64, 70, 87t;
Mary Evans Picture Library 21t; Fox Photos 67,
81, 87b; Horse & Pony 65; Ed Lacey 27, 28
colour, 34, 35; Leslie Lane 10, 25, 29, 37, 56, 75,
88; Mansell Collection 20, 21b; Monty Photo-
graphy 74, 82; Picturepoint 68 colour; Pony &
Lighthorse 11, 22, 42, 44, 54, 72, 73; Potomac
Equestrienne Centre 85; US Equestrienne
Team 84; Robert Estall 57b

© Macmillan London Limited 1973

L.C. Card 73-14096

Design by Paul Watkins & Florianne Henfield

Illustration Research by Susan Mayhew

Drawings by Joan Thompson & Jacqueline Wright

Phototypeset by Oliver Burridge Filmsetting Limited,
Crawley, Sussex
Printed in Japan by Dai Nippon Printing Company

ISBN 0-690-00446-X

1 WHAT'S IT ALL ABOUT?

As a leisure activity, riding has become more popular throughout the world in the past twenty years. Whereas riding for pleasure was once a pursuit of the wealthy, it is now enjoyed by anyone who wishes to learn the art of horsemanship, whether to a high enough standard to eventually take part competitively, or simply to enjoy the unrivalled feeling of freedom that this sport can give to the most novice riders.

Riding can be taken up in almost any country in the world and, within reason, by virtually any age group. This then is a major attraction of the sport when compared with so many other leisure activities which may involve coping with the ardours of spending hours in a soaking wet condition in a boat, or with the hardship and physical effort of climbing. Given a suitably tempered horse or pony, anyone who is able to actually get on their chosen mount will be able to amble happily around the riding school enclosures before being escorted out on a ride to explore the country from a previously unknown vantage point.

One reason for the upsurge in interest in riding as a participant sport, especially in the British Isles, has been the influence of television. The excitement of competitive riding comes into the home, and a whole new field of sport has been opened to the previously non-riding public. Although few spectators have aspirations to become international stars in the show-jumping and three-day event world, the inescapable lure to try and master the art is there. And so the prospective equestrian proceeds to the local riding school in his first attempts to acquire the neces-

sary skills to keep himself and his horse together. It cannot be stressed too strongly that the major factor in successfully learning to ride is to find a reputable establishment with qualified instructing staff and well-kept horses. Far too many are badly run, the horses are used like machines and the whole set-up smacks of a factory turning out a set of inexperienced riders every hour to take their chance in the open country or, worse still, along busy roads with the added hazard of impatient traffic.

Dangers

Riding can be a dangerous occupation if the rules are not observed. No-one would get straight into an automobile and expect to drive off without some form of prior instruction and an accompanying qualified driver to sort out problems as they arise; but all too often a complete beginner is hoisted, somehow or other, into the saddle and expected to follow the school ride as they set off for their hour's exercise, more often than not, at that most uncomfortable of all paces for a beginner, the trot.

A horse is a potentially dangerous form of conveyance in the hands of a complete novice and as well as being a risk to the rider, can cause untold damage if permitted to do as he pleases. For a complete beginner therefore it is imperative that the first lessons are given under strict supervision and that confidence between horse and rider is established from the earliest contact between the two. A horse is a sensitive creature and can immediately ascertain whether the rider is nervous, which, quite naturally, the majority of beginners will be. However, the best schools will contain a certain number of patent-safety horses or ponies who are thoroughly reliable and completely unworried by

A lesson in progress at an indoor
school. Strict supervision during
lessons is an essential ingredient of
learning to ride if the beginner is to
progress

the antics and activities of their new riders. Even when faced with
the most confusing instructions, these faithful servants will continue to plod co-operatively around the school until the beginner
reaches some form of understanding with his mount. The building
of confidence between the horse and rider is the first step for any
instructor with a new pupil. Once destroyed, by an unnecessary
fall perhaps, the confidence of a beginner is difficult to re-
establish, as every move the horse makes seems to herald
another painful and traumatic incident as the rider makes contact
with the ground.

Attractions
A great attraction of riding as a leisure sport and a healthy
activity is that it can be enjoyed by individuals and does not
require the presence of other people. It can, of course, be equally
enjoyable when shared with a crowd of fellow riders, but there is
no reason why a solitary rider should not set off on his own
(provided of course that he has had the necessary grounding in
basic instruction) enjoying the sport to the maximum. The company of other riders and horses can also be enjoyed, and many
horses will perform more satisfactorily if taken out with others.

As modern-day travel becomes faster and easier, so ideas and
habits spread to different countries. The British Isles has a long
history of riding which has been passed on to some of the more
recently developed countries. As international riders travel the
world competing with one another, so more and more people take
up the sport of riding as their chosen leisure activity. As communications improve, it is possible to read about and see other
countries following this sport in their own particular way. Methods

vary from place to place, but the basic reason is much the same all over the world—a love of animals and a wish to learn how to ride in order to emulate some famous personality or star in the horse world, or simply to take one's exercise in a way that is both pleasant and healthy.

After a time spent learning the basic principles at a recommended school, the pupil will begin to progress. Although most riding schools will always try and provide a suitable horse for hire, these become slightly mechanical in their actions as they are constantly being ridden by different people. As the rider progresses he will find that his scope becomes severely limited in all but the really top-class training establishments. In such a school, he will be able to progress on to the more testing horses and will automatically become more ambitious and eager to improve his ability and knowledge.

Riding can and does become something of a disease; those

who become afflicted eventually come to the decision to buy their own horse. To keep to the minimum of expenditure, the straight answer as to whether or not to purchase a horse is 'no'. Many people find that riding once or twice a week at a school is all they require of the sport. And this involves a known outlay in the cost of lessons and basic equipment. But once they have embarked on the ownership trail, the expense begins and is unending.

So, wherever you live it is possible to take up riding and, on the other side of the coin is the spectator aspect of this sport. As more and more publicity is afforded to the competitive horse world, so more and more people, who would be no more likely to sit astride a horse than fly to the moon, are taking an avid and ever-increasing interest in riding by watching others competing.

Watching population
It is estimated that a large number of visitors to the top-class shows and events will never have, or for that matter never want the opportunity to sit on a horse and learn to ride. They are the watching population who enjoy seeing others take part in their favourite sport. As international competition increases and press and television coverage grows, so the number of people who go to shows grows too. This is more true in the British Isles than in any other country in the world. Distance plays a large part in this story. Whereas in the United Kingdom, riders and spectators can choose from a mass of shows and events running continuously from March to October within easy distance of almost any point on the compass, the North American continent and Australia have to cope with vast mileages in order to travel to competitions. Consequently, unless the shows are held in large cities, attendances are far smaller when compared with the numbers watching and riding in the UK.

Part of the appeal of riding is the relationship between man and beast. For many who have had little or no contact with the animal world, it can be a rewarding experience when contact is made with a living creature who can provide so much pleasure and enjoyment, in return for which he asks nothing but to be fed, watered and cared for in a humane manner.

The fact that a trained horse is dependent on the human race for his survival opens up an entirely new dimension in the field of human experience. Unlike a tennis racquet or a golf club, a horse cannot simply be put away for a few weeks and then brought out when next required. He needs constant attention. There is little in the world of sport that can compare with a carefree ride in beautiful surroundings and the fact that the horse is obviously enjoying itself too, can only add to the pleasure. For some people, riding may be the only way of getting away from the ever-increasing turmoil of everyday life.

Children and the handicapped

Riding gives enormous confidence to children. It encourages independence of character since understanding a sensitive animal requires tact and patience. It also requires determination to improve and encourage the horse to do what is demanded of it by the rider.

Riding has also opened up a new dimension to the handicapped.

For children and adults who are physically handicapped, riding can enable a previously closed world, that of moving about unaided, to be re-opened or even experienced for the first time. The horse provides the legs and in a short time, the previously chair-bound individual is able to take part in an occupation that will bring him on equal terms with his more fortunate physically fit companions.

Although methods may differ round the world, the basic aim of horsemanship is the same wherever horse and man are found working together. Since the demise of the real working horse with the introduction of the internal combustion engine, horses have carved a new niche in the modern world: that of a provider of pleasure for millions of riders and non-riding enthusiasts many of whose lives depend on the horse as a means of living. No other sport requires quite the same degree of attention to the essential piece of equipment—and it is this thought that should be foremost in the intending rider's mind. Also, one can never stop learning, and this is another great attraction. As soon as one particular aspect has been mastered, another problem seems to appear on the horizon and there is a never-ending quest for improvement and more knowledge.

Riding in towns
It is also worth remembering that riding is not confined to those

15

Previous pages: A group of American
riders out on a trail ride. There is little
that can compare with a carefree ride
in beautiful surroundings

Below: Not everyone has the
opportunity to ride in the country.
Many people spend their time riding in
built-up towns and cities
Right: A ride preparing to leave the
yard from a stables in suburbia

who live in country surroundings. Obviously, riding over open
land through woods or over the prairies is infinitely preferable to
an hour or two around a city park—but many riders have no choice
and it is a common sight in several big cities or built-up areas to
see parties of riders jogging gently round the marked out tracks.
This may seem boring to the rider who is used to endless miles of
country bridle paths, but for the city-dweller it gives ample
opportunity to enjoy a little freedom. But too often a lot of town
riding schools have to use the main highways and roads before
reaching their riding areas. Nevertheless, judging by the strings
of horses and riders seen, especially at the weekends, walking
contentedly along the roads, the philosophy is clearly that to be
riding at all, even if not in an ideal area, is better than no riding.

When a particular sport is the chosen pastime of a public figure,
interest in that sport will quite obviously increase. And so it has
been with riding. Princess Anne has shown the whole world that
she is capable of doing something really well in her own right and
not simply because of her position. She has proved that by hard
work coupled with a natural talent, it is possible to rise to the very
top of the equestrian world. Her success and her achievement in
being the Champion European three-day event rider have provided
the best possible advertisement for riding as a sport and have
encouraged spectators to turn out and watch events in their
thousands. Although riding is enjoyed by over a million people in
the British Isles, the publicity created by Princess Anne has
certainly encouraged others throughout the world to take up this
rewarding pastime.

2 A HISTORY OF RIDING

It is thought that the horse first became part of man's domestic scene in about 1700 BC. Evidence suggests that wild horses inhabited only Europe and Asia and it was not until less than 4,000 years ago that man began to realize that the horse could assist him in his struggle for existence. Whereas man first looked upon the horse as a source of food, gradually he came to realize the potential of this versatile animal. First of all, most probably, as a draught animal faster than cattle, and eventually as a means by which man went to war, hunted, and travelled from place to place. Eventually the horse must have been seen not only as a driving animal but as a form of transport faster than any other previous methods. From that time until the present day, the horse has been the partner in a unique association with man.

The first evidence available that shows man actually riding good horses comes from Egyptian history in the 14th century BC. But no saddle had yet been invented which must have made the control of a high-spirited horse a matter of some chance, not to mention the risk involved. However, several archaeological discoveries show that the Assyrian warriors used saddle cloths which would have afforded a little more grip between horse and rider. A far cry from the sophisticated and expensive equipment with which we adorn our horses today.

The first riding master to make an impact on the world and to leave a record of his teaching was the Greek horseman, Xenophon. Still without the use of a saddle with a tree (the basis of the modern saddle) the Greeks and other horsemen rode either bareback or on a variety of padded saddle cloths. Nevertheless, the position taught by Xenophon was to remain the orthodox riding seat for European horsemen until the 20th century. Xenophon rode and taught his pupils to ride with a long almost straight leg. This method still survives in the 'western' style of riding. It is easy to see how riding simply for pleasure would have followed automatically for the soldiers and warriors, as Xenophon made his men practise by riding across country negotiating any obstacles in their way. One can imagine how this type of exercise would soon become a form of recreation as young horsemen raced each other across country. Not such a far cry from present-day point-to-points. The Greeks enjoyed flat-racing and Xenophon was a keen hunting man. Much of this early master's sage advice still applies to this day. Perhaps one statement well worth remembering is 'Never lose your temper in dealing with horses'. This will always remain a sound piece of advice for anybody in contact with horses.

Following Xenophon and his teaching, equitation as an art did not appear to develop much over the next few centuries. But during the first century AD, an important invention, destined to have a major effect on riding and the use of the horse, appeared on the scene. The introduction of the horseshoe meant that a horse could be worked on hard and stony ground without harming the sensitive and all-important foot. The shoe as we know it today, has altered very little. It is still made, in most cases, of iron and it is nailed to the hoof by attaching nails to the dead part of the horny hoof. Recently there have been various attempts to change the style and material of the heavy shoe, but so far none of the new ideas have really replaced the original model.

Then there are the mythological stories of horses that have intrigued so many people for centuries. The horse has always held a special and relatively exalted position in the imagination. And in practical terms too, man has to literally look up to a horse, unlike his other domesticated animals, the dog and the cat. But with a horse it is different. Considerably bigger, heavier and decidedly stronger, the relationship between man and his horse must be one of mutual trust and respect, for man is unable to master a horse with sheer physical strength. In short man and horse have to reach a compromise. The horse is willing to act as servant in return for very little by human standards—merely to be fed, watered and generally cared for.

Because man is subservient he has, either consciously or subconsciously, elevated the horse to the realms of gods and goddesses. One of the best-known legendary figures, Pegasus, the winged horse, was invested with powers beyond those of any earthly horse. But a winged horse was only a short step from some of the fleet-footed steeds known to the Greeks, and this was an example of how highly the equestrian race was held in awe by a mere human being. The Greek sun god, Helios, had a team of four fiery horses symbolizing the orbit of the sun through sunrise —Erythraios; the dawn—Aithon; brilliant mid-day—Lampos; and the sunset Philogaios.

Greek mythology tells us that Poseidon, the god of the sea, was responsible for the creation of the horse, and the horse and water were inextricably linked in the minds of the Greeks. After Pegasus came the creature that was half man, half horse, known as a Centaur and this being was thought to have originated in fountains. Bellerophon, said to be the son of Poseidon, was given Pegasus as his mount and this combination achieved fantastic success in the battlefields; after all he had an undeniable advantage in that he was able to take to the air to avoid trouble. A similar situation can be imagined if, say, Napoleon had been equipped with a vertical take-off jet or a helicopter at one of his battles. But the triumphs of the warrior Bellerophon came to an end when he attempted to fly Pegasus upwards towards the gods. Zeus dashed him to the ground and death for his presumption.

It was not only the Greeks who deified the horse. The Chinese, whose holy books show that some form of equitation may have been in evidence in 2155 BC, thought very highly of the horse. Later on the Chinese participated in race riding on saddles with

Right: The father of equitation—
Xenophon—the Greek riding master
whose theories and teaching are still
relevant today

Below: Two Etruscan winged horses.
These statues were harnessed to the
chariot of a god and made around
300 BC

Right: Chinese jade carving of a horse's head. The early Chinese thought very highly of the horse and produced many works of art to represent their prized creature

Below: Some of the earliest records of man actually riding a horse come from the Egyptian paintings often found in the tombs of the pharoahs

A champion Arab stallion, Darjeel. The influence of the Arab on breeding stock has spread to most countries of the world as he imparts stamina, speed and undeniable beauty to his offspring

high back rests and short stirrups. This was similar to the great natural horsemen of the Mongolian plains today.

Perhaps one of the best-known legends associated with horses is that of the Arabian Bedouins who believed that God created the horse from the southerly wind:

'When God decided to create the horse, He spoke to the southerly wind: "Condense thyself, for of thee I shall create a new being in honor of My saints and to the humiliation of My enemies."

The southerly wind spoke: "Create it then, O Lord." And God took a handful of southerly wind, blew His breath over it and created the horse.'

Seeing some of the most beautiful Arabian horses today, especially against their natural background of the desert, it is easy to imagine how this legend originated.

It is not often realized that although horses exist today in all corners of the world, the equine race originated in the northern areas of Europe and Asia. Their spread over the continents has been partly due to the movement of man during wars and in search of new territories, and partly to natural migration. Now, of course, horses are transported all over the world in order to introduce new strains and blood lines into established stock. Few countries have escaped the influence of the Arab and the English thoroughbred and it is on these two types that most of the world's horses are now based. The link may be very distant but in most

of the breeds, it is usually possible to trace the ancestry back to one of these foundation stocks.

To many, the horse is the most beautiful creature in the animal kingdom—he is a creature of many different moods and the legends and poetry surrounding him are numerous. Without the presence of the horse throughout history the story of mankind would have been a vastly different one. 'Our history was written on the backs of horses. Never was there an animal as completely involved in the service of man as the horse. And never have gentleness, obedience and devotion been so ill-rewarded. Yet, never has greater distinction or similar glorification been accorded any animal. The history of man reveals the heritage of the horse. Memory will not keep silent. We are his heirs, even if today we believe that we have no further need of him.' A similar passage which is traditionally read at the closing ceremony of the Horse of the Year Show in London every year expresses even more clearly the nature of the horse:

'Where in all the world is nobility found without conceit?
Where is there friendship without envy?
Where is there beauty without vanity?
Here one finds gracefulness coupled with power
and strength tempered by gentleness.
A constant servant, yet no slave.
A fighter ever without hostility.
Our history was written on his back.
We are his heirs.
But he is his own heritage, the horse.'

In these few moving words, we see the horse described in all his moods, and there can be no doubt that this sensitive creature fully lives up to this description.

And so from the slightly misty records, the role of the horse and the art of horsemanship are gradually presented in an altogether clearer picture as records covering the last 2,000 years are more reliable.

As we look at the history of the horse, first as a source of food, then as a means of transport, for hunting and in war and exploration, we eventually arrive at the present day where the horse, as we know it, is used mainly as a source of pleasure and relaxation. Although in some parts of the world, such as Australia, and America, the horse is still very much part of the working scene. Here he is used for shepherding and driving cattle and still fulfills a need that cannot be replaced by the internal combustion engine in all its sophisticated forms. Other countries also employ the horse in a working capacity.

Police and ceremonial horses are not just part of the English scene, they also feature in other parts of the world; the Canadian Mounties, the Swedish Household Cavalry; the police horses in Jordan and many others still serve a useful and often unique

purpose. There is something awe-inspiring about a large, strong four-legged beast bearing gently down on one as the police horses firmly push a mass of people in the required direction. The action of the police horse is often far more effective and less likely to cause enraged violence than the use of a motorised vehicle or armed policemen on their own two feet.

There will, of course, always be the hooligan element who will try and inflict injury on the horses in an attempt to prevent them carrying out their job. It says much for the forbearance of these animals that in spite of being exposed to all types of disturbance they go calmly and quietly about their task and do not refuse to keep up their good work when their rider demands an extra response. When half a ton of horse firmly places his hoof on your toes, you are left in little doubt as to which way to move.

The accolade for the turn out and performance of ceremonial horses must, without doubt, fall to the United Kingdom. One only has to attend a ceremony such as the Trooping of the Colour on

Left: In certain parts of the world the horse is still very much part of the working scene. Here in Australia, horses are used to help round up stock in the outback

Another horse who works hard and uncomplainingly for man. The Police Horse of the Year, Sandown. Police horses are trained to a high degree to ignore all types of disturbance and carry on with their work

Horseguards Parade to appreciate the standard set in this field. But many other countries keep stables full of horses in their capital cities either for the police force or the cavalry regiments, or both. Some of these stables have their origins in the old cavalry schools, which were the teaching centres for the art of riding in the army. Schools such as the Spanish School in Vienna, the Cadre Noir at Saumur in France still exist today but, alas, the British army no longer has Weedon, the centre in Northamptonshire where cavalry officers were once trained in all the equestrian skills. However, the United Kingdom is well-supplied with privately owned schools that exist throughout the length and breadth of the country.

From Xenophon until the middle ages the art of classical riding progressed little. Indeed it is probable that all that was required of a horse was that it should walk and gallop in a straight line to enable the knights of the middle-ages to compete in their tournaments. However as war became more sophisticated with the invention of small firearms, it became imperative for horse and rider to be able to manoeuvre in a more agile way. In the late 15th and early 16th centuries the art of classical riding became part of the European life and the great cavalry schools sprang up.

In 1532 the first modern school was established in Naples by Federico Grisone who based his teaching on the works of Xenophon. Classical riding then spread to France where Antoine Pluvinel de la Baume, a student of the Naples school, was appointed equerry to the Duke of Anjou. Pluvinel then established a riding academy in Paris and wrote his book *La Maniege Royal* (1632), while giving instruction to the future King of France, Louis XIII. The French master's methods in schooling his horses were vastly different from those of his Italian instructors. Pluvinel believed in obedience from his horses through gentle but firm discipline, rather than by force and violence.

At the beginning of the 17th century England too was giving birth to her first recognized school of riding. William Cavendish, Duke of Newcastle was born in 1592. Although another Neapolitan student, Chevalier Saint-Antoine had begun teaching in England, Cavendish began his riding career by setting up a riding arena in Antwerp. Returning to England when Charles II was restored to the throne he was then created Duke of Newcastle. His chief book *A General System of Horsemanship in All Its Branches* (1658) contains an account of all the experience he accumulated whilst on the continent. Meanwhile in the other leading European equestrian countries, Spain, Germany and Austria, classical riding was finding its beginnings. 1572 saw the first documented reference to the 'Spanish' Riding School in Vienna. The prefix Spanish arose because of the origin of the horses used in Vienna, and has no connection with the style of riding adopted in Spain. And so this, probably the most famous riding academy in the world, has continued to command the highest respect for its standard of teaching in the art of classical equitation.

It is interesting to see the increasing attention given to schooling horses to a standard for competitive work in the dressage field. More and more people are becoming involved in the dressage world as the ordinary horse owner learns to understand more about this difficult art. Dressage, or the training of the horse, is beginning to lose its aura of mystery. Although obviously it needs specialist training and many years of endless practice to achieve the standard required in top-class dressage, there is a better understanding among the everyday riders and these are the people who are striving to school their horses accordingly. Riding a well-schooled and obedient horse brings far more pleasure than careering around the countryside at an uncontrolled, and, more often than not, uncomfortable pace. Modern training centres spring up like mushrooms in different countries and these will be dealt with in more detail in a following chapter.

3 INTERNATIONAL SCENE

Most sports produce their own celebrities and the equestrian world is no different in this respect from football, tennis, motor racing or any other closely followed spectator sport. Over the past twenty years the racing and show-jumping worlds have been subjected to a lot of publicity and this has resulted in personalities emerging who are treated in much the same way as film stars and other internationally known figures.

These stars were making their mark in their own particular sphere well before the newspapers and television put them in front of the public eye, but their exposure through the mass media has resulted in the ordinary man in the street taking an interest in all forms of horse sport as both a spectator and a participator. Actual participation in riding, which involves getting astride a horse and learning how to stay there before progressing on to further lessons, has become so popular as a leisure pastime that stables are under considerable pressure to provide enough facilities to cater for the demand.

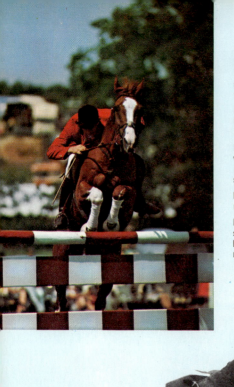

Previous page: The incomparable
Arkle with Pat Taafe in the saddle,
sailing over the water jump in typical
style. Arkle had a star-like quality,
which added to his outstanding ability

Left: The World showjumping champion
David Broome on Mister Softee at
Hickstead

Below: The near-legendary Pat Smythe
with Flanagan. Her rise to fame was
instrumental in the increased interest
shown by the non-riding public

Right: One of the best American lady
riders is Kathy Kusner

Below right: One of the outstanding
show jumping personalities of today,
Harvey Smith riding his 1968 Olympic
mount, Madison Time

The blue riband of flat racing is the Derby, run at Epsom, England in June. The best 3 year olds battle for the coveted title which can mean a small fortune for the owner of the winning horse

Riding differs vastly from most other sports in that few boring preliminaries exist—you go along to the school and before you know where you are, a horse or pony has been produced for you out of a stable and you are being taught how to get on. Maybe it is a pretty shaky start but to hear a class of beginners discussing their early rides, you would imagine that they were well prepared and ready to tackle anything in their path.

In other sports such as ski-ing or tennis, it takes a long and often boring time before one reaches the standard where one can join in with others. But with riding, after one or two lessons, most beginners are quite capable of joining a quiet ride in company with others.

It is very easy after watching the top professionals like flat-race jockey Lester Piggot, to imagine yourself galloping freely across the open countryside, because there you are, actually on a horse and looking remarkably like your favourite idol. Of course, the chances of a beginner ever reaching the standard of the top-class jockeys are remote, to say the least, but some do aspire to these heights. The most that the majority of learners want out of this unique sport is to be able to ride confidently round the country, perhaps popping over one or two small obstacles and maybe to take part in local competitions. There is always encouragement as you watch a well-known competitor jump an immaculate round over a huge course of fences. Next time you visit the stables your imagination may run away with you as you progress happily round a relatively small set of fences, but the thrill will be there just the same.

Another reason why riding is such a popular pastime is the involvement with a living creature. The British people especially are extraordinarily fond of animals and although one may never possess an Arkle or a Nijinsky or a Stroller, one's own particular favourite can mean just as much as these high-priced and famous horses. Your own horse may not have quite the ability or he may not have such a distinguished family record. But even if he only achieves minor success at the smallest of gymkhanas, it will seem just as important to you as a win in the Derby or the Grand National does to the owners and riders of top class stock. There can be little doubt that the present upsurge of interest in riding has been due mainly to two factors—one being the enormous publicity given to international racing and show-jumping since the war and the increase in leisure time for most people. In the British Isles over two million people now take part in various equestrian activities. This is a two hundred per cent increase in twenty years and the growth of the Riding Club and Pony Club movements are clear proof of this fact. The Pony Club flourishes in many different countries and does much to start children off in the correct manner in both riding and horse-mastership. As well as teaching a child to ride and helping him to improve his pony, the Pony Club lays great emphasis on the care of the animal itself.

Riding presents a complex picture because so many people take part in so many different ways: some own their horse; others ride animals belonging to friends or to riding establishments. It may be a highly organized activity or simply a casual pastime: it may involve those who still require horses as part of their working life as in Australia or America where horses are still used extensively for ranching sheep and cattle; or in countries where horses are kept for ceremonial or police work; it may be competitive or non-competitive. It is interesting, therefore, to look at the competitive and highly professional world that exists in many countries as the standard and frequency of events has much influence on how much riding goes on among the once-a-week riders.

Racing
There can be little doubt that the most important section financially is to be found within the racing world. Every year the bloodstock sales in the leading countries attract buyers who are prepared to pay vast sums for prospective flat race winners. The financial return on a big race winner does not end with the prize money. Stud fees that can be demanded for a top-class proven stallion can be phenomenal and may well run into millions of pounds or dollars for the owner. And then there is the glamour and thrill of racing and of seeing your own colours being carried by your horse.

Racing throughout the world attracts thousands of spectators and followers who have an in-built love of the racing scene and, of course, gambling. Thousands who are fanatical racegoers will never have the opportunity, or for that matter want to ride a horse themselves. Except for a few the vast majority of racing supporters are unlikely to get nearer to a horse than when they are leaning over the paddock rails watching the runners parade.

But there is a magic attraction attached to these beautiful horses—the thoroughbred has taken generations to produce and few people appreciate the years of hard work, care and thought that have preceded the breeding of these exquisite creatures. Bred for their stamina and speed the sight of a field of eager, fit racehorses has little to equal it and more than repays the years of dedication that have been spent before the end product is achieved. The complete uncertainty of the racing game (horses are unpredictable creatures) adds an extra touch of excitement and risk to this fast-moving sport.

What goes to make a really top class jockey, like Lester Piggot? Or his equally gifted predecessors like Sir Gordon Richards, Fred Archer, Steve Donoghue, Scobie Breasley from Australia, and Tod Sloan, from the United States, who introduced the forward racing set now used by jockeys the world over?

The legendary Archer who rode 2,748 winners in the 19th century, Sir Gordon Richards (4,870) who is now a top-class trainer and Steve Donoghue are all names that spring to mind as one watches the jockeys of today. Jockeys begin their professional lives as apprentices in racing stables and it is soon clear who will eventually reach the top. They are necessarily small in build and light in weight and they could never hope to hold an impulsive and strong young colt by sheer strength and brute force. It is here that tact, understanding and sheer riding skill come into their own. And it is not just in racing that this applies.

No-one can control a horse's strength by force. Control is achieved by a mutual understanding between horse and rider and so one of the first requirements of a good horseman is tact coupled with patience and a feeling for the horse to enable him to communicate his wishes by aids. Aids are the signals given to the horse by the rider by hands, legs, body and voice and provided the aids are clear and the horse has been schooled to respond to them, he does as his rider asks when required to do so.

The basic attributes of any top-class horseman or woman are the same: an affinity for and an understanding of a highly temperamental animal; tact and patience in order to deal with a mentality rather similar to that of a young child; dedication to long hours of hard work in schooling horses, covering the same ground over and over again in order to teach an unruly pupil elementary lessons, and finally, that certain something which is a gift when dealing with horses. Also important is a co-ordination of mind and body that enables the rider to see ahead and make plans to avoid pitfalls that the horse cannot comprehend. It is often up to the rider who may know, for instance, that a wide ditch lurks on the landing side of a seemingly innocuous fence. It is only by preparing the horse for an obstacle such as this that a major disaster can be averted. By walking round a course before competing, the rider can gather information as to the best route to follow to enable his horse to negotiate the obstacles safely. Without this prior knowledge, there can only be grief in store for both horse and rider. With this knowledge, the rider will not be frightened. If he is while on the back of a horse his fears will communicate themselves to the horse who will react accordingly. Confidence between horse and rider is absolutely essential.

Show jumping
When one looks at a list of well-known personalities, so many of these qualities are apparent. Take for instance the world of show jumping. David Broome is the world champion and he has the gift whereby he can establish a rapport almost immediately with almost any horse he rides. He is renowned for dealing not only with problem horses. Often horses that had shown a marked dislike for show jumping before Broome rode them, became top money winners in the international field. He is such a totally sympathetic rider that the most headstrong horses go quietly and generously for him.

When Broome won his world title in La Baule in 1970 he had to ride three strange horses as well as the notoriously difficult Beethoven. His handling of all four animals showed his particular skill at its best in that he achieved the best overall score. Since that event he has proved that it was no fluke as he has won several similar competitions. A truly great rider, brought up in Wales riding ponies as a child before graduating to adult competitions, he has won two bronze medals at Olympic Games and has been the backbone of the British international show jumping team for the last decade. His popularity is apparent when one sees the endless queue of fans wanting his autograph at the shows. David Broome has one gift that all horsemen covet, what is known as 'hands'. This one word means that his control of his horse, which is partly achieved by contact through the reins to the horse's mouth, is a model of sympathetic handling. A horse's mouth is a sensitive structure and it is only by the action of good hands that the messages transmitted to the horse are clearly understood with the minimum of discomfort.

Good hands are born, not made and untold damage can be wrought by a rider with bad or 'heavy hands'. Whatever the situation, David Broome's handling of his horse is a model for all aspiring riders to follow. Broome and his contemporaries Harvey Smith and Anne Moore may be the stars of the moment, but show jumping owes a great debt to some of the earlier campaigners who graced the international arenas in the fifties.

The name of Pat Smythe is almost legendary. The near fairy-tale story of a young girl's rise to fame in what was very much at

The individual show jumping gold medalist at the 1968 Olympic Games, Bill Steinkraus of the USA on Snowbound. Steinkraus is also a talented musician

that time a man's world, caught the public's imagination. It is probably this one rider more than any other person, who was responsible for the sudden interest in competitive jumping. Pat Smythe appeared on the scene just as television was getting into its stride and it is her early battles at the Horse of the Year Show in London that many people still remember. Brought up to ride anything, rather like David Broome, Pat produced her own string of internationally successful horses and became the first woman to win an Olympic medal for show jumping. Her story has been told in full in best-selling books and she started a tradition of lady riders in Great Britain that has gone from strength to strength.

It is the one sport in which women compete on equal terms with, and with equal success against their male counterparts. This, too, may be part of the attraction of the sport—certainly for the women—to actually compete against and beat the men.

The United States
The list of celebrities is long, but to turn to an American, whose style is possibly the best to be seen in the show jumping arena, we come to Bill Steinkraus. With five Olympic Games to his credit, Steinkraus rode Snowbound to win the individual gold medal in Mexico in 1968, narrowly defeating the fantastic pony,

Hans Winkler has been Germany's outstanding rider for two decades and is
equally successful at home and abroad.
Here he is riding Enigk, at the Mexico
Olympics in 1968

Stroller ridden by Marion Coakes. Steinkraus is a product of the
training of the United States Team trainer, Bertalan de Nemethy,
a Hungarian who has been the architect behind the American
show jumping successes. It is interesting to note that Steinkraus,
like David Broome, Harvey Smith and Pat Smythe and other top
riders from different countries achieved his success with a
variety of horses.

Germany

The most successful show jumping nation in terms of Olympic
wins is undoubtedly Germany. Four team gold medals since 1956
is an amazingly consistent record and the Germans have a
seemingly unending supply of top-class international horses.
Their outstanding rider has been Hans Winkler, individual gold
medal winner in Stockholm in 1956 and a member of the German
international team for many years. But he does not have it all his
own way. Schockemoehle and Shridde, Steenken and Wiltfang
constitute a formidable challenge and between them take many
of the major prizes at international shows. The German method
of riding and schooling is markedly different from other countries.
Their horses are mainly bred from the big Hanoverian strain
which is a breed possessing enormous power in the hind

quarters, so very necessary for a successful show jumper. The Germans are strict disciplinarians and all their horses receive a very thorough schooling on the flat before being put over obstacles. This devotion to basic ground work continues through-out their jumping career. One only has to watch the German competitors schooling or 'riding their horses in' before a big competition to appreciate how much emphasis is laid on this aspect of training. And this schooling pays dividends as can be seen from their record at the Olympic Games and at the inter-national shows.

Dressage
Germany also produces some of the finest dressage competitors in the world. Again, the dedication of horse and rider comes to the fore, although some people prefer to see the more free-going forward action of some of the other horses rather than the highly-disciplined, faultless, but sometimes stilted action of the German horses. They occasionally lack the brilliance and gaiety shown by their rivals, but they are deadly accurate and precise in their movements and gain many marks for that part of their per-formance. Dressage has for many years filled most people who ride for pleasure with untold fears and apprehension.

The very mention of the word 'dressage' at a Pony Club rally was, until fairly recently, enough to scare away all but a very few. It seemed to conjure up the idea of an elegant horse and rider performing the most complicated and advanced movements in a flower-bedecked arena, watched by an admiring and knowledge-able audience. But basic dressage is really another word for schooling one's horse to be obedient at all times. Fortunately much has been done to dispel the old fears and the interest has increased as more people begin to take part in elementary competitions. The intelligent rider realizes that a well-schooled horse presents a much more pleasant prospect as far as enjoy-ment is concerned. As more and more riders take an interest in dressage, so the standard will steadily improve at all levels.

Dressage is an important factor too, in the horse trials or eventing world. The first phase in an event consists of a dressage test varying from the novice standard to the FEI International Test for full scale three-day events. Combined with the speed and endurance and the show jumping phases the dressage forms an integral part of the competition.

In the early days of horse trials, one could perform a mediocre dressage test and then make up valuable marks by flashing round the cross-country, but this is no longer the case. A good test is now essential in most events, although some people, notably the Australians, still manage to do well at international level with what can after be described as 'interesting' per-formances within the confines of the dressage boards. This

HRH Princess Anne and Columbus
showing a well-balanced and rhythmic
turn in a dressage arena. Dressage is
becoming far more popular as the
mystique and secret fears are dispelled

Josef Neckermann, riding Antoinette. He is one of Germany's leading dressage exponents. A perfectly balanced horse, performing a series of movements in response to its rider's aids, is a sight well worth watching

nation's performance across country is usually of a very high standard and they manage to pick up enough bonus marks to cancel out their dressage penalties.

Provided one has a simple basic knowledge of a horse's action and paces, dressage can be one of the most interesting and beautiful sights for the spectator. Over the last few years, much has been done to educate the vast audiences watching the major shows, by a discreet commentary on exactly what horse and rider are attempting to achieve. The sight of a perfectly balanced and schooled horse performing the specialized movements at the

lightest aid from his rider is well worth watching, especially when one remembers the patience and hard work that have gone into producing the end product. To train a horse to Grand Prix standard which is the level of training required for the Olympic Games, can take anything up to six or seven years of progressive education. This is undoubtedly why dressage has not attracted masses of active followers in the past. One has to have a very long-term view to consider this type of training. Nevertheless it is encouraging to see the increasing interest in this side of riding. There is of course as in all branches of riding, a lack of sufficiently qualified instructors and judges, but the national bodies are fast recognizing this and courses and seminars are run in order to train more people for these tasks.

The handful of top instructors throughout the world are always in great demand to take courses, and they frequently travel overseas to lecture and teach besides travelling the length and breadth of their home country. As interest increases, so the demand on the instructors becomes greater and it is difficult to keep pace with the growth of this side of the sport. With dressage, it is particularly important to have someone 'on the ground' to point out your faults and help correct the errors in the movements.

As communications and transport become more efficient, so riders are able to exchange ideas, compete against each other and generally publicize a previously neglected branch of equestrian sport. This will result in a general improvement in the overall standard and knowledge in the field of schooling horses. It cannot be stressed too strongly that this side of equitation is for everybody, and not only for the experts at the top. Schooling a horse is the equivalent of teaching a child good manners and is an essential part of the education of the equine if it is to be a pleasing, safe, and above all enjoyable ride.

Although celebrities in the dressage world do not hit the headlines with quite the same impact as jockeys, show-jumpers or three-day event riders, there are those who have caught the public eye. One of the best loved, certainly in Great Britain, is the 70-year-old grandmother who came twelfth overall in the Munich Olympic dressage. Mrs Lorna Johnstone, who celebrated her 70th birthday during the 1972 Games, has produced a great number of top-class dressage horses. Her placing at the Olympics behind the immaculate German and Russian contingent was just reward for her efforts over the years. The two German riders Liselott Linsenhoff—gold medallist in Munich and Josef Neckermann (bronze medal) have between them dominated the European dressage scene for some years, but the Russians are equally well represented and carried off the team medal in Munich. The Russians still have a great deal to learn in the show jumping and eventing world, but their dressage performances are well in advance of most other countries.

Polo is probably one of the oldest
games to be played on horseback.
Because it is expensive to play its
appeal is to the spectator rather than
the participant

As riding becomes increasingly international, riders in different sections learn from one another and those in training for international team events can do this, especially where dressage is concerned as all three Olympic equestrian sports require the basic knowledge that can be provided by a dressage trainer.

Polo
Yet another side of the international scene covers the activities on the polo ground. To play polo at competition level is very expensive. It is really a spectator sport and attracts large crowds throughout the season. Probably originating in Persia, polo is one of the oldest games on horseback. It spread to the western hemisphere via India during British rule. It is now played extensively in the United States and also in the Argentine where many of the best polo ponies are still produced. Some of the world's finest players come from the Argentine and many of them spend most of the time playing in the top British or American teams. British players have improved over the last ten years or so mainly because of the influence of the Pony Club who have helped to encourage young players. American teams make frequent visits to England for raids on the high goal tournaments. They may base a lot of expensive ponies at one of the big polo centres, such as Cowdray in Sussex or Cirencester in Gloucestershire, and then play in the open tournaments organized during the summer. The coveted Cowdray Gold Cup is the prize they are after, but in 1972 it was retained by a British based team.

As polo is so expensive to play few can afford it. A large measure of its popularity has been due to the interest and active part taken by HRH the Duke of Edinburgh. A first class player, he did much to bring the sport to the notice of the public. Although he has now given up playing due to a recurring injury, his eldest son, the Prince of Wales, has also developed a keen interest and shown considerable talent on the polo field. It is an exhilarating, fast-moving and often dangerous sport for riders and judging by the crowds attending, it is almost as exciting for the spectators.

As international competitions continue to increase so the non-rider is attracted to the sport. In order to cater for this popularity new centres are being set up in Britain. Local authorities are realizing the need to provide riding facilities when they are considering setting up amenity and leisure areas.

There are many other aspects of the competitive scene which do not attract the same degree of international attention, but are nevertheless an integral part of the riding world. Many of these tend to be restricted to certain countries—bronc riding in North America and Canada, gymkhana events which figure in many countries but do not constitute an international sport as such; showing horses—also predominantly restricted to individual countries. These will be dealt with in later chapters.

4 WHERE DO I START?

For many beginners, the first problem they will have to face will be the choice of a suitable establishment. With the increase in interest in riding there has been a corresponding expansion in the world of riding establishments. Of course much will depend on the beginner's eventual target and ambitions when he sets out on his newly-discovered sport. Many will be happy simply to learn the basic rudiments to enable them to enjoy a weekly ride while others will have their sights set far higher and will obviously require a wider range of instruction and a more varied choice of horses to ride.

Riding schools
To find out whether the local riding school is capable of providing the type of instruction required, the complete novice has three choices: he would be well-advised to consult the national organization, who may be able to assist in the choice of stables; or he can ask a more experienced rider to advise on teaching facilities in the area; or, and this method is not to be recommended, he can proceed to the local stables and try them out for

himself. The last choice involves a tremendous risk—a complete beginner can have no yardstick by which he can assess the standard of his chosen school. There are, unfortunately, far too many stables that do not come up to even the minimum standards required.

If the beginner, therefore, ventures forth on his own he may not only be disappointed but also may be put off riding for life. Often to the totally inexperienced eye, some of the worst establishments may seem adequate to the beginner when in fact they are badly run with worn-out horses who are under-fed, badly shod, or occasionally not shod at all. If a stable cannot afford proper instructors, the horses and ponies are often kept on minimum rations so that they behave in a docile manner with complete beginners and children. The unsuspecting clients are hoisted up on a dejected-looking animal who can often only just manage to shuffle out of the stables, plod aimlessly around the local paths with little life and return his rider safely to the yard.

It is fairly obvious that the first step for the beginner must be to seek advice. Even if the local riding school is close at hand it is

often better to travel a little further afield if you wish to get complete enjoyment from riding, and, furthermore, value for the money you are paying in order to learn to ride. To pay a small sum simply to sit on the horse's back for an hour is a waste of good money. Riding is an expensive sport and there is little point in spending the money unwisely at a poor stable before finding out the drawbacks. It is better to pay more for the chance to learn properly from the beginning. Half an hour with a really good instructor can be worth more than all the time spent trying to find out for yourself exactly how to cope with your horse.

So the first step must be to find a well-run school which is going to provide the facilities you require. Some stables do little other than teach the basic skills and cater for ordinary riding, or hacking, as it is called, in the surrounding countryside. For those who are slightly more ambitious they will find schools specializing in competition work while some stables will cater for all branches of equitation at all standards. Another word of warning—a new school may look to be the most efficient and obvious place at which to begin one's riding career but all too often the outer sparkle covers up an inexperienced stable and it is often the smaller, less ostentatious places that offer the most to the beginner. So it is important not to be deceived by external appearances although, of course, it is equally true to say that a badly kept, dirty and untidy establishment will not offer a suitable service either.

But the beginner can only learn about standards by practical experience. The standard of teaching is of prime importance as the early lessons can do much to create a real love of riding. So before booking into the school, make quite sure that the staff are both qualified instructors and good at their job. Again it is often a case of trial and error. What may suit one person may be all wrong for the next. Personalities can clash and if the beginner finds himself at odds with his instructor, he should change as little progress will be made.

A school may claim in its advertisements to carry a staff of

qualified instructors, when in fact they may be so busy schooling and competing on the stable horses, that the actual teaching becomes neglected and in some cases non-existent. This is obviously a useless state of affairs where the beginner is concerned and he would do far better to choose another stable where the necessary individual attention can be found.

Basic equipment

So, having chosen your riding school you enrol for a course of lessons and then, before you actually begin, you have to kit yourself out with the necessary equipment. Riding a horse is not like riding a bicycle or learning to drive an automobile. Certain articles of clothing are necessary for both comfort and safety. There has been a radical change in riding wear in the past few years and the majority of articles can be afforded by most people. Obviously one can embark on a terrific spending spree and purchase a complete riding outfit from one of the well-known suppliers. But to start with this would seem a little extravagant. First discover whether you really intend to carry on with your chosen sport, then if you really are keen, by all means go ahead and buy all the correct clothing. But until then, it will be far wiser to stick to a simple wardrobe and keep the initial expense to the minimum.

The prevailing climate will influence the type of clothes you buy. In a hot country the minimum amount of heavy material will obviously be the sensible choice, whereas in Britain winter riding can be one of the coldest outdoor pastimes and it will be absolutely essential to have wind and waterproof clothing.

The first and most important articles to be purchased are head and footwear. It is these two pieces of equipment more than any other that can spell the difference between safety and disaster. A hard hat is usually velvet covered, reinforced and therefore acts as protection to the head in the event of a fall onto the hard ground. This can be purchased for a sum around £5 (around $11), although the price can vary greatly. But as long as the hat fits comfortably

Clothes

1 Leather hunting boots. A similar shaped boot can be purchased in hard rubber. 2 Hard, velvet-covered hunting cap or riding hat. The most popular form of protective head wear.

3 Jodhpurs—normally made in a stretch or cotton fabric which is easily washable. 4 The short jodhpur boot, most useful for the weekend rider as it is much cheaper than a full length boot

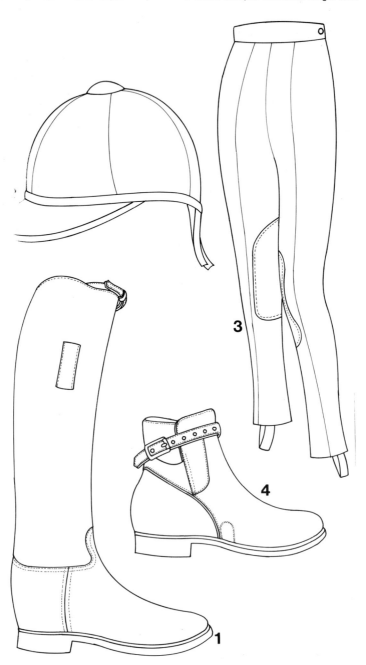

and well, there is no need to spend huge sums of money on the individually tailored article. There are also several varieties of fibre glass and hard plastic crash helmets on the market. These are similar and in some cases identical to those used by jockeys and can mean the difference between irrevocable brain damage and mild concussion.

Jockeys know how hard they can hit the ground while travelling at speed and there is always this risk when riding. You may not have intended to be moving quite so fast when you fall off, and falls are inevitable when you start to ride and for that matter whenever you ride, but you are riding a sensitive animal that will occasionally do something unpredictable. It is at moments like these when a hard hat can make all the difference. Also, it is useless to wear a hat on some occasions and leave it behind on others. Nine times out of ten, the day you leave it at home will be the day you have an accident. It is a mark of a good stable that they insist that *all* their clients *and* staff wear hats at all times when mounted. So stay away from a school where you see some with and some without hard hats.

As far as footwear is concerned, it cannot be overemphasized how important this is to ensure maximum safety for the rider. Again there is no need to go to vast expense to purchase immaculate leather hunting or 'top' boots. There are jodhpur boots which can be purchased for a reasonable sum, again in the region of about £5 ($11). These have smooth leather soles, and a good well defined heel, to prevent your whole foot from slipping through the stirrup iron. A fairly recent innovation has been the hard rubber riding boot, which is a long calf length boot. These should not be confused with wellington boots which have a heavily ridged sole that can be exceptionally dangerous as it can become stuck in the stirrup iron. The hard rubber riding boot has an almost smooth sole designed to act in the same way as a leather sole. They cost about the same as jodhpur boots and are extremely easy to keep clean as they only need to be washed off after use. You will often see the most amazing footwear adorning the feet of some riders, but again in the interest of safety and comfort there is no replacement for the proper article.

So now you have your head and footwear settled. The next article is the type of trouser. To sit on a relatively hard leather saddle in which you will be constantly moving can be an uncomfortable experience if your legs are not properly protected. Until the beginner is riding in the correct position there is the risk that the skin will be rubbed by contact with the saddle unless he wears the right type of garment. There is a vast selection of different materials and designs on the market and once again the climate will have considerable influence on the choice of material and style.

Tight stretch breeches or jodhpurs (the difference between

these two is that breeches finish just below the knee and are worn with long boots, whereas jodhpurs extend right down to the ankle and can be worn with short jodhpur boots) are fine in a temperate or cool climate but can become unbearable in the warmer countries. A cotton or natural fibre material is usually the answer where the temperature tends to rise. Alternatively many people find they can ride comfortably in a tough pair of jeans or slacks, although they have to be chosen with care so that they fit well and do not bunch up round the legs leaving a vast expanse of unprotected skin.

One or two firms produce a denim-type trouser designed expressly for riding with reinforced areas in the parts that tend to take the most wear, such as inside the lower leg and on the seat of the trousers. The advantage of this casual riding wear is that it is both inexpensive and hard wearing. As long as you look neat and clean there is nothing against wearing this type of ordinary trouser. Obviously breeches and jodhpurs look better and personally I find them more comfortable to ride in, but there are plenty of others who find the casual clothes more comfortable.

It is important, however, to be comfortable in the clothes you choose as the resulting agonies from rubbing against the saddle can be enough to put the keenest beginner off riding for all time. Perhaps the least important area of clothing is that worn on the top half of the body. Again depending on the climate, this will consist of cotton shirts, polo necked sweaters and some form of wind and waterproof jacket. There are many highly suitable anorak-type garments that are ideal for riding in all weathers. Their only disadvantage is that they do not cover the legs in heavy rain. The advantage of an anorak is that it can be used for everyday wear as well as riding, whereas if you purchase a tweed riding jacket it is probably expensive and will only be suitable for riding.

Gloves are an optional item of equipment. I wear them most of the time and they are essential in cold and wet weather when reins can become slippery and almost impossible to grip without gloves. String gloves in yellow, white or fawn are popular, they wash easily and grip wet, slippery leather. Again there are many types that vary in cost, material and weight. Some are wool-lined or have rubber grips attached to the fingers. The important factor to remember is that they should not be too bulky as this will hamper your handling of the reins, which will only lead to difficulty in controlling your horse.

As the beginner becomes more experienced he will probably want to spend more money and purchase more sophisticated equipment. A recent innovation has been the introduction of a safety harness that ensures that the hard hat remains on the rider's head during a fall. All too often in the process of falling, the hat flies off and is, therefore, less than useless. To overcome this there are various attachments that are strapped on to the hat or built in to the inside. A strap fastened under the rider's chin means that the hat stays in place even when the rider is upside down. Various arguments periodically arise in relation to the use of this type of harness. It is rather similar to the controversy surrounding the use of car seat belts. In the end the decision must rest with the individual but it is worth trying this type of hat before making a final choice.

Fashions in riding clothes will obviously vary from country to country but basically the idea is the same—comfort, and protection for the various hazards that are always present in the world of riding. Besides being comfortable and safe a rider should attempt to look clean and neat. Long hair should be tied back at the nape of the neck for casual riding. A famous hunting personality once said 'Long hair is for the ballroom'. For showing or hunting, hair should either be secured in a neat bun or braid, tucked right inside the hat or held secure by a strong hairnet. In cold weather frozen ears can be prevented by wearing a thin headscarf underneath the hat.

For hunting, shows and western riding, the correct attire should be worn and this means a much larger outlay in expenditure so if you intend to progress to the hunting field and the show ring, be prepared to spend considerably more money.

For example if you intend to hunt there are certain rules of etiquette and fashion which must be observed before you can join the followers of your chosen hunt. As a member of the 'field' (the term given to all those, apart from the hunt servants and Master or joint-Masters, who follow hounds) you will be expected to turn out in one or other of the accepted forms of dress. It is best on these occasions to ask the advice of a seasoned foxhunter who knows the form where hunting is concerned. It is both bad manners and impracticable to arrive for hunting in the wrong attire and although some hunts will allow a slight relaxation in this sphere, others may well send you home for being improperly dressed.

Hunting clothes were, in the main, designed for very good reasons. For instance long boots made of tough hard wearing leather protect your legs against protruding branches, tree trunks, gate posts or from getting badly injured from a kicking horse. They are also of infinite value when you have to dismount in a muddy gateway. A strong jacket protects the upper half of your body against tearing thorns and brushes as you ride through them, probably at a fairly fast pace. Your hunting whip helps to ward off swinging branches from your face as well as acting as a gate opener and shutter, besides the traditional use to help collect hounds together. So hunting dress is not simply a matter of 'looking the part', there is a practical reason behind the wearing of the kit. Equipment for the horse will be dealt with again in Chapter 5.

5 LEARNING TO RIDE

You have chosen a suitable school and purchased your riding gear. You are now ready for your first hour of instruction. For someone who has previously had no contact at all with horses, the instructor should explain one or two elementary terms before beginning the lesson. It is nerve-wracking when, as a complete beginner, you are brusquely told that 'your mount is tacked up in the box waiting for you'. What on earth does it mean, you ask yourself? Is your horse waiting for you, nailed up in some large box somewhere? No, it means, in fact, that your horse has already been equipped with his saddle and bridle (tack), and is waiting in his stable.

I think a beginner should be shown round a yard, have the basic items explained and be shown exactly how the saddle and bridle are put on. Too often instructors take it for granted that their pupils understand all the terms used. Why not start at the beginning and explain the simple facts? It is up to the rider to ask the questions. If he shows himself willing to learn and shows an interest in the horse and equipment, he will gain far more from his lessons. Prior instruction will help, especially when the rider is advised to adjust a piece of equipment such as shortening or lengthening a stirrup leather, or to tighten the girth. If he already knows how to do this before actually getting on to the horse, he will not search hopelessly in complete confusion.

So possibly the first part of the early lessons will teach you how to handle your horse and its equipment. As well as being useful to know these facts, this initial contact can help to instil confidence in a beginner. If the stable allows you to do so, try and observe and learn about how the horses are handled and looked after. Too many beginners have one idea in mind—to get on to a horse and gallop off at high speed. Any stable that permits a client to do this should be avoided. Often, the preliminaries may seem a little monotonous, but experience shows that those who try to run before they can walk (literally) usually come to grief before long.

If you have chosen well for your place of instruction, you will be given a quiet and entirely reliable horse or pony, depending on your size and weight, on which to begin your first lessons. These may be given either in an indoor school, a large covered building with an artificial soft floor, or in an outdoor marked-out area known as a manège. A good stable should have either of these facilities. If not the first few lessons may be taken out on a ride on the leading rein. In this case the instructor will ride alongside the pupil with a rein attached to the pupil's horse and will have control.

The first lesson will consist of instruction in mounting and dismounting and you will then be shown the correct position for actually sitting in the saddle. You will be told how to position your legs and feet and how to hold the reins. Once in the right position the instructor will explain how to give the simple aids in order to

Mounting and dismounting 1 Stand by the horse's shoulder facing the tail, and holding the reins in the left hand. 2, 3 and 4 Place left foot in stirrup iron, left hand on the front (or pommel) of the saddle, right hand on the rear (cantle) of the saddle, hop and spring from the right foot and swing right leg over the back of the horse. Take care not to thump down heavily into the saddle or to dig the horse in the belly as you get on with your left foot.

5 Dismount by quitting both your stirrups. 6 Swing the right leg using your hand as a pivot on the horse's withers. 7 Spring lightly down to the ground keeping hold of the reins

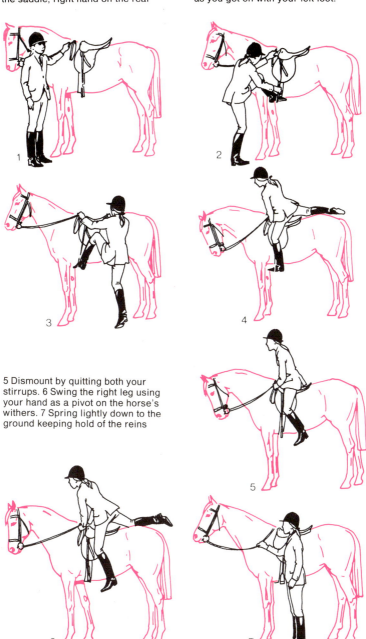

Position
The correct position in the saddle—
seat bones well down in the centre of
the saddle, heels down, toes forward,
head up and elbows in

Holding the reins
Here the rein is held between the fourth
and fifth fingers, but this is not a rigid
rule

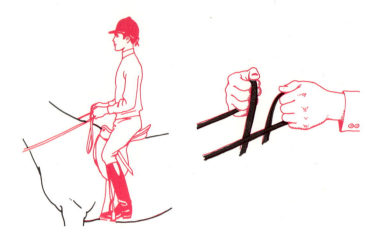

make the horse walk forward. This will be ample for a beginning,
but you may also be required to do one or two easy exercises in
the saddle to help improve your balance.

This may all sound very elementary, but it is surprising how
few people realise what is entailed in actually achieving results.
After the initial lessons the rider should overcome the first
inevitable feelings of losing balance and being in a slightly
precarious position. Progressive lessons will follow with the rider
learning how to cope with the faster paces of trot and canter.
Once the instructor is confident that his pupil is reasonably safe
and confident in the saddle, he may begin to ask for more
advanced exercises while in the saddle, not only in the stationary
position but while the horse is on the move. Designed to improve
the balance and position of the rider, these exercises are in-
valuable in producing a rider whose 'seat' (the term given to the
position in the saddle) is independent of his hands. In other
words, the pupil will not feel the need to 'hang on' to the reins in
order to keep his balance.

Some instructors may put the horse on the lunging rein, a long
rein attached to a special bridle by which the instructor controls
the horse while it circles him at the various paces. The rider can
then give all his concentration to performing and perfecting his
lessons while the instructor copes with the horse.

As you progress, the school will provide more horses for you
to gain further experience. The greater variety of horses that you
can ride, the better, for it is only by riding different animals that
you gain in experience and learn how to deal with different
situations that may arise.

Not everybody who learns to ride wants necessarily to learn

Exercises

Exercise in the saddle help to improve the position and seat of the rider. Standing up in the stirrups without holding on to the reins or a neckstrap is good for balance as is the swinging of the arms. Riding with the stirrups crossed improves both position and balance

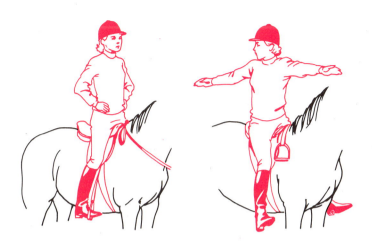

how to jump, but sooner or later the opportunity will arise. Provided the beginner has developed a firm seat at all paces and has achieved the balance necessary to adjust his position to the horse's movement, small obstacles can be tackled. By small, I mean really small to start with. Nothing more than poles on the ground and the first lessons are usually carried out over several poles laid in a line known as trotting poles. These may then be raised to a maximum height of about eighteen inches and are termed cavaletti. Once the instructor thinks his pupil is advanced enough, he will then be allowed to tackle proper obstacles if he so wishes and will soon be negotiating small natural obstacles such as ditches and low rails while out on a ride.

Buying your own horse

The time will come after a series of lessons when the rider may begin to consider purchasing his own horse.

The most important question is, can you afford the financial outlay and regular expenses involved? Have you somewhere suitable to keep the animal in winter and summer? The back garden and the garage simply will not do. Horses have large and constant appetites and are gregarious creatures. They pine for company if not used to being kept alone and demand attention seven days a week, fifty-two weeks of the year. Are you prepared to ride in all weathers, break the ice on a sub-zero morning on your horse's water trough, cart loads of fodder down to an inaccessible field and do a thousand and one other things that will arise as soon as you have your own animal? If the answer to any part of these questions is 'no' or even doubtful, don't consider owning your own horse. Without adequate facilities, the only

As lessons progress the pupil will soon find himself able to negotiate small natural hazards such as ditches and water. Such obstacles will add to the variety and enjoyment of the ride

result can be a disastrous one for both man and beast and you will be far happier riding week by week at your riding school.

First decide what you want to do with your horse and what you want to be able to use him for. Do you simply want to continue to ride around the countryside, popping over the occasional jump or do you want to go a little further and compete in small, local shows? Maybe the idea of hunting attracts you. The price of the horse will vary greatly depending on your requirements. It is almost impossible to fix a price you will have to pay as the value of horses at the present time varies so much that any figure quoted will rapidly be out of date. It is enough to say that a good, honest, sound horse will not be cheap.

The nine breeds of native pony found in the British Isles are especially popular and in great demand for children, as many of them make ideal mounts for young people. By interbreeding Arab and Thoroughbred stock with New Forest ponies or the Welsh Mountain pony for example, a really lovely child's pony has been produced. The resulting offspring will combine many outstanding features of both breeds. The hardiness of the native breed with the beauty, speed and performance of the blood lines produces a beautiful animal. Little wonder that British ponies are to be found the world over giving immense pleasure and satisfaction to their owners.

For a small lightweight adult, some of the bigger native breeds such as the New Forest, Connemara, Highland or Welsh Cob can provide all the answers and many are bought as 'family' ponies as they are equally capable of providing fun for adults and children. One of the main advantages of buying a horse or pony with a large proportion of native blood in its veins, is that it will be far easier to keep as far as feeding and care are concerned.

Not everybody who learns to ride will want to jump, but early lessons will be over mini-sized obstacles so as not to overface horse and rider

A bigger, thoroughbred type of horse will need much more attention especially during the winter months, whereas the cross-bred will probably be able to live out all the year round and not require as much exercising or concentrated work. With the ever-increasing demand for ordinary riding horses, the prices inevitably increase. So it is often difficult to find exactly what you want at a realistic price and you may have to overlook one or two minor faults in the horse in order to get anything that is reasonably priced. But I should stress again that it is imperative to enlist the help of an expert when purchasing a horse and also to instruct a veterinary surgeon to give the horse the equivalent of a thorough 'medical' in order to check for any disabilities or signs of unsound-ness. The vetting of a horse is essential as there is no point in finding yourself with a horse you cannot ride because it turns out to be lame and therefore useless. A few pounds spent on this exercise is money well spent and can save a lot of disappointments.

All this may sound depressing. Don't be discouraged but take all these precautions. An inexperienced buyer should stay well away from public horse sales. Only the most knowledgeable people can hope to find anything worth buying, and they, too, often come to grief. Horse sales should not, of course, be confused with the regular bloodstock sales that are held during the year at the various racing centres. These are very different and attract the racing fraternity. It is here that the world's bloodstock are bought and sold.

The only way to purchase a horse is either by word of mouth or to search through the advertisements in the equestrian journals. There are, too, reputable horse dealers who keep a stable full of horses for sale and this can often be the right answer for the

Native breeds

Below: The Welsh Mountain pony on his native Welsh hills. One of the smaller native breeds, but very strong, hardy and beautiful

Below centre: The Connemara pony is one of the larger native breeds in the British Isles. Easily capable of carrying an adult, it is extremely hardy and will live out in all weathers

Bottom left: The stocky and immensely strong Highland pony, still used to carry loads in the Highlands and popular as a trekking pony because of its sure-footedness on stony mountain paths

Below: The New Forest ponies are always popular with children
Bottom: The Appaloosa or spotted horse of the Americas. Once the prized mount of the Nez Perce Indians and now a popular riding horse in the USA

beginner. Remember it is better to go for the slightly less handsome model who will probably cater very well for your requirements. It will also be much cheaper.

The financial side of keeping your horse must be carefully considered. As already stated, keeping a horse is not like keeping an automobile. A horse requires constant attention and if you are not prepared or cannot afford to give him this attention, do not consider keeping your own animal. However, if you do not want the responsibility of keeping the horse yourself, and you can afford the added cost, the answer is to keep your horse at livery at a reputable stable. This has many advantages in that if you have a full-time job, and many people who ride are in this position, your horse is always ready for you when you want to go for a ride and is looked after by the staff at the stable. The term livery is applied to stables that care for horses belonging to clients who pay an agreed price each week for the keep of their horses. The price will vary—some stables offer full livery, which means that your horse will be exercised for you if you cannot get to ride him on some days, he will be fed, mucked-out and groomed for you and made ready whenever you want to take him out yourself. It is impossible to state a standard fee for this type of service, but it is unlikely to be available for less than £10 a week as an average and some stables will charge considerably more than this. The equivalent service in the United States is termed 'boarding' and again the cost will vary greatly from one part of the country to another. Prices will range from $65 a month to maybe as much as $200.

If you are prepared to do some of the work with your horse, such as exercising, grooming, and all the other chores, the fees for livery will be correspondingly lower as all the stable will be providing will be fodder and accommodation. However this type of arrangement needs to be worked out carefully between the parties concerned. Some stables use some of their liveries for other clients by arrangement with the owner, but in my opinion this is not a satisfactory arrangement. If you have your own horse you don't really want total strangers riding it and perhaps upsetting it in one way or another. It is better to have perhaps one or two members of the staff at the stable looking after your horse and exercising it. In this way you know far more about his condition and well-being. Please also remember that the livery fees only include the services already mentioned. On top of this you will have a regular blacksmith's bill, cost of buying and repairing your equipment, possible veterinary bills, insurance fees, travelling costs if you hire transport to and from a show or a hunt, competition and hunting fees.

If you are lucky enough to have your own facilities for keeping a horse then your costs will obviously be considerably less. The back garden or small orchard are not adequate facilities. At least

A lesson in grooming for a group of
Pony Club members. Grooming is an
essential chore if you consider keeping
your own horse. It must be done
regularly to keep your horse in a fit
and healthy condition

an acre per horse must be allowed and this will have to be rotated
during the year as horses need to be taken off a pasture for periods
of time to allow the grass to recover. Ideally therefore you need
two grazing areas so that you can move your horse from one to
the other at intervals.

He will also need some form of well-built shelter, even if he is
going to live out all the year round. The chances are that he will
spend more time in the shelter during the hot summer months to
escape the nuisance of flies and other insects, than he will in the
coldest winter weather. If you can arrange to share grazing with
another horse owner, so much the better. Horses enjoy each
other's company and if left alone, they will spend a lot of time
hanging about by the gate waiting for company to arrive, either
equine or human. Even if you have your own grazing or rent it,
your costs will still be quite substantial as your horse will need a
daily feed and hay during the winter months as well as feeding in
the summer if you intend to work him fairly hard. The price of
feeding stuff and equipment continue to rise and must also be
taken into consideration. Too many horses are kept under bad
conditions. Their owners expect to be able to ride their horse hard
all over the weekend and then neglect him for the other five days.
Riding an unfit horse can only mean eventual disaster and
disappointment. It is far better to save your money and continue
to ride at a stable as your horse will soon become an expensive

Saddles

1 All Purpose	4 Racing
2 Jumping	5 Western
3 Dressage	

liability and a chore, and remember, your riding is meant to be a leisure activity and provide relaxation and enjoyment. So unless you are prepared to devote a considerable portion of your time and money to him, it is not worth considering the purchase of a horse of your own.

Basic equipment

However, if you decide to buy your own horse you will also need to purchase various basic articles of equipment before you can start riding. Sometimes it is possible to buy your horse fully equipped with saddle, bridle, rugs and other items. This is not always the case, so I will give some idea of the requirements for the new horse owner.

A saddle, preferably of the type known as all-purpose or general purpose. These are self-explanatory and are designed for the maximum comfort for horse and rider in all branches of equitation. They can vary in cost from about £35 or $100 to £120 or $400 for a good German or French saddle. A saddle must also have a girth, the strap which passes under the horse's belly and secures the saddle to the back of the horse. Girths can be made of a variety of materials, some suit some horses, while others don't. Materials used are leather, string, nylon, elasticated and ordinary webbing.

For ease of care I recommend a nylon girth, although they do have a fairly limited life. Stirrups and stirrup leathers are of mainly uniform design, but I would advise the purchase of a pair of rubber stirrup treads or pads which fit into the stirrup and prevent the sole of your boot slipping around when muddy conditions prevail. The size of the stirrup iron is also important as too large or too small an iron can be very dangerous in the event of a fall. If the iron is too large, your foot may slip right through, and if too small, your foot may become stuck in the iron and you run the risk of being dragged if you fall off and your foot is not released.

Ask for expert advice when fitting the saddle and make sure you know how to put it on so that it is comfortable for your horse with no bits of skin pinched together. If this happens the result may be a spectacular buck when you get on to your horse. It is most important to keep all your saddlery immaculately clean for two reasons. One is that if you allow dirt to accumulate, this will eventually rub the horse and cause sores in the most inconvenient places. Secondly, leather will soon become brittle and crack, eventually breaking at the most inopportune moment. This can be both expensive to replace and extremely dangerous if the break occurs while you are riding or perhaps jumping. A third very good reason for keeping your tack clean is that nothing looks worse than dirty, unkempt equipment. It is an insult to your horse and is comparable with going out in dirty, grubby clothes yourself.

Your choice of bridle and bit will depend on the type that has been used before on your horse. Many varieties are available.

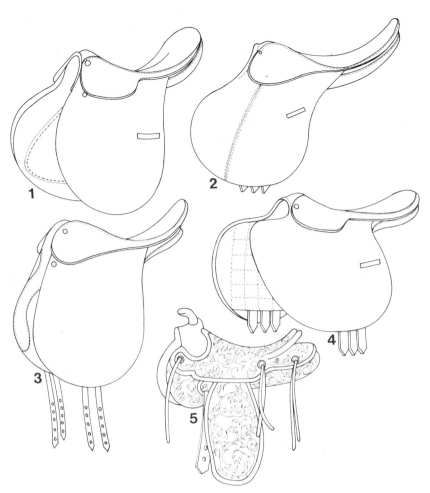

1

2

3

4

5

Again expert advice should be sought if you are in any doubt as to what you should use. A horse's mouth is an extremely sensitive area and his performance will depend much on what type of bit you choose and how you use it.

As well as a saddle and bridle, you will need a head collar and rope or chain for tying your horse up for grooming and other chores. A leather head collar is best although there are now nylon and plastic varieties that are cheaper and wear well. A set of grooming tools are essential for you to be able to keep your horse's coat in a clean and healthy condition. A grooming kit should consist of the following articles: a hoofpick for cleaning out your horse's feet; a stiff dandy brush to remove mud and sweat from the coat; a body brush (which has softer shorter bristles) to clean the coat, remove the dirt and scurf and to stimulate and massage the skin; a metal curry comb to clean the body brush as it is used; a water brush to damp the mane and tail and to wash the feet; and a mane comb for occasional use on an unruly mane and sometimes to untangle the tail—but the body brush should normally be used; sponges for cleaning eyes,

Bridle
1 A double bridle 'Put up'
2 A snaffle bridle 'Put up'
3 Leather head collar
4 American-style

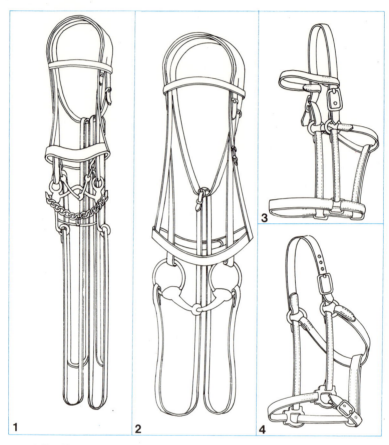

nostrils, lips, dock and sheath; and a stablerubber (rather like a large tea cloth) to wipe over the coat at the end of grooming. Grooming tools should be periodically washed through in much the same way as you would wash your own hairbrush and comb. They should be kept tidily in a plastic bucket or canvas bag and I have found it a good idea to attach a long coloured string to the hoof pick, as this article has an annoying habit of finding its way into the bedding in the stable, and this can save many a frustrating hour sifting piles of straw searching for the missing object.

A set of tools and wheelbarrow (which can do double duty in the garden if geographically possible) will be needed to muck out your horse's stable. Even if you do not intend to keep your horse in a stable constantly, the occasion will arise when you will need to give him a bed of straw, or whatever bedding you choose, and then the stable will need cleaning out. A fork, broom and shovel

Grooming kit
1 Hoof pick
2 Water brush
3 Body brush
4 Curry comb, (for cleaning body brush during grooming)

5 Mane comb
6 Dandy brush
7 Stable rubber

are all that is necessary—you can in fact make do without a wheel-barrow by using an old sack split down one side and piling the dirty bedding on this. You will also need a feed bowl or bucket as well as two buckets for water. A hay net to save wastage of this expensive commodity is also essential. The money spent on a net will soon be saved by the economy in wasted hay. No horse owner should be without a simple first aid box containing some disin-fectant, a thermometer, scissors, cotton wool, gauze bandages, gamgee tissue, crepe bandages, Vaseline, carbolic soap, cough electuary (paste), liniment of some type and some anti-bacterial powder. It should be remembered that only the slightest injuries should be treated at home, anything other than these necessitate the vet, as an anti-tetanus injection may be needed if the damage is serious. Materials for cleaning your tack are saddle soap, sponges, metal polish, dusters and polishing rags and some type of softening oil.

You may or may not need rugs and bandages (other than first aid bandages) depending on whether you intend to travel your horse or clip his coat in winter. It is, in any case, advisable to have some type of rug to put on your horse in the event of illness as he will need to be kept warm. A jute night rug lined with wool will be quite sufficient.

One of the most useful is the type that looks like a string vest and is a great help in drying off your horse when he has become wet either from sweating or from weather conditions during work. This is a very good investment and will save a lot of time and effort at the end of a long hard day. If like many owners, you find you want to clip your horse during the winter to enable him to do fairly hard work, you may decide to use a specially designed rug known as a New Zealand rug. This is made of waterproofed canvas lined with wool and equipped with special straps so that the horse can move freely round his field and roll.

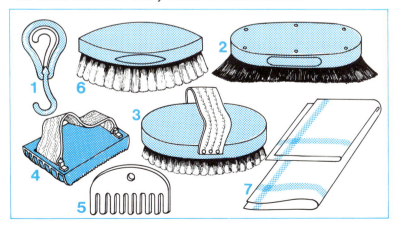

6 OPPORTUNITIES TO RIDE

Once you have completed a course of lessons, the number depending entirely on how each individual progresses, you will begin to feel far more confident and to think about the numerous opportunities open to you now that you are capable of controlling and enjoying your horse.

A lot will depend on the type of stable you have used and on the area in which you ride. Obviously if your chosen stable is situated in a very built-up part or even in a town, the scope will be limited However, even riders in London manage to find the odd little diversion in Hyde Park although obviously nothing can compare with the chance to ride in the wide open countryside. The only answer is to travel out of the towns and possibly take lessons in a less highly populated area. But not everybody can do this, so the rides in Rotten Row in London and in Grand Central Park in New York are the only answer.

In London, riders are not neglected. Several riding clubs and branches of the Pony Club arrange their events within reach of the inner London stables and one of the high spots on the calendar is the London Riding Horse Parade held annually in Hyde Park. Anyone who keeps or rides a horse in the Greater London area can compete in a variety of riding classes—some of which are judged on condition of the horse and turnout of horse and rider, while others cater for ladies riding side-saddle and teams of three from licensed riding establishments. The parade is organized under the auspices of the Greater London Horseman's Association and the event is designed to encourage a high standard of turnout and to promote the welfare of the horses and ponies kept in the London area.

It is often something of a surprise to learn that about 30,000 people ride horses in the London area every week and the horse population in Greater London is somewhere around 5,000. This includes those belonging to 75 licensed establishments as well as those owned by costermongers, rag and bone men, breweries, British Horse Society riding clubs and individuals. Riding within the confines of a town may not, at first sight, appear terribly attractive, but judging by the number who choose to do it each week, it clearly has plenty to offer.

Of course the stabling and keep of a horse in a built-up area presents huge problems, so in the main most of the riding is done from established stables. There are other outlets besides actually riding for the horse enthusiast based in a town. Although nothing can really substitute for riding a horse, there are evening classes run covering the art of horsemanship. Lectures are given by personalities from the horse world and demonstrations in some of the big London indoor schools are well patronized. Some of the large companies and organizations such as the Civil Service and the BBC have their own Riding Club which provides facilities for those working and living in London. Some town-based clubs arrange to visit other clubs that are situated in the country, and members from cities take part in some of the club activities on horses borrowed from members of the host club. As demand increases, so more stables are set up within easy reach of the big towns. One such example is in the Lea Valley just north of London, where the Regional Park Authorities have decided to include a riding stable in the leisure facilities to be provided in the 10,000 acre park.

A major step in enabling townspeople to ride has been the introduction of riding to the timetable of some London schools. Not only riding, but instruction in stable management is given and these all help to introduce a new and fascinating sport to young people who otherwise might not have had the opportunity to get anywhere near a horse, let alone learn to ride.

So much for riding in the towns, which although greatly enjoyed by those who have little opportunity to ride elsewhere, can never really compare with the unrivalled feeling of freedom and independence experienced when one is riding in the country. The United Kingdom is fortunate in having an almost ideal climate and some of the finest riding country in the world in which the enthusiasts can enjoy their sport to the fullest extent. Other countries may experience far more violent extremes of temperature and some months of the year may make it climatically impossible to ride all the year round. In the main however, riding is a sport that can be carried out in most weathers. There is little to compare with an early morning ride with a light fall of rain, a mist rising off the fields and the promise of 'rain-before-seven, fine-before-eleven'.

The prevailing climate in each country will obviously have a considerable effect on the type of riding activities that are popular

Rodeo riding is a popular sport (mainly spectator) in North America. This has sprung from the everyday work of the cowboy, who still functions on some of the huge ranches

in different countries. The terrain too, will have its effect. So in the United States and Canada with the thousands of square miles of vast, open uninhabited spaces, the pursuit of trail riding is one of the more popular forms of equestrian sport. Summer camps are held from which base riders go out all day exploring the magnificent countryside of the Canadian Rockies or through the national parks. The United States offer wide variety in the field of camps and riding holidays for those keen to spend a fixed time with their horses and the organization of these camps is conducted at a high standard with facilities for all grades of rider. A similar service is offered in the British Isles at the pony trekking centres and some stables who specialize in riding vacations. But there is no real equivalent to the long trail rides organized. Pony trekking can often simply be a means to admire the scenery from a different vantage point, and it does not always fulfil the client's wish to enjoy all-day rides. Indeed, it can frequently be an uncomfortable experience if the centre is not carefully chosen. The magazine *Horse and Hound* issues a long and comprehensive list of establishments offering a variety of 'horsey' vacations, but the centre chosen should always be checked if possible before a vacation is finally confirmed.

Many pony trekking centres are situated in some of the most beautiful scenic areas such as the Welsh Mountains, the Lake District and the Scottish Highlands and the West Country moors. There can be little doubt that it is one of the finest ways of seeing the countryside and with the minimum of effort. It should be remembered that the majority of pony trekking will be conducted

Trekking has become a favourite
equestrian past-time in many countries.
Riders in Arizona have the chance to
admire the magnificent scenery

at the slower paces of walk and trot, so if you are hoping to be able to have a real *riding* vacation with plenty of variety, rather than a scenic tour, trekking is not really the answer to your vacation question. A good and reputable trekking centre will have a Certificate of Approval issued by the society known as the Ponies of Britain.

Trekking is certainly the answer for some of the older beginners as it is essentially a fairly sedate occupation and will also be emminently suited to those who prefer to hack gently around, and do not require the thrill and excitement provided by jumping and more advanced forms of riding. Before spending a week or fortnight in which you will be doing nothing but riding all day, it is advisable to try and get as fit as possible, for even if you ride regularly once or twice a week, the effects of spending a whole day in the saddle can be excrutiatingly painful.

Long distance rides

There has been, in recent years, a rise in the popularity of long distance rides and endurance rides in the British Isles. This is a well-established branch of the equestrian scene in North America since it was adopted by the US Cavalry in the 1920s. They sponsored five-day 300 mile rides and nowadays some of the most famous endurance rides consist of 100 mile trails. These distances require all-round horsemen who are capable of producing horses fit enough to complete the distance in a set time. Shorter rides are organized too, for those who do not have the time to prepare for the really gruelling events. In Great Britain, the idea has taken hold and the Golden Horseshoe Ride consists of a 75 mile ride spread over two days.

Many clubs run rides of varying distances, not necessarily as competitions, but often to introduce riders to new paths and to show them the network of local bridleways that are available. As these rides become more popular, so bridle-paths are linked to provide longer and uninterrupted rides. A fine example is the recently opened South Downs Way that runs the length of the Sussex Downs to the Hampshire border. This is both a footpath and a bridleway and provides riders with the opportunity of keeping off the dangerous and unpleasant roads and away from the heavy traffic. British riders probably suffer more than most in their traffic hazards, and for this reason it is most encouraging to see local authorities making provision for riding as they plan their new leisure areas.

While on the subject of bridle-paths it is of vital importance that these paths remain open and passable in all weathers and at all times of the year. As this is in the best interest of riders it involves what is known as bridle-path clearance. Many paths have become overgrown and completely impassable. In order to combat this, groups of keen riders and non-riders for that matter, spend some

A group of riders on a French beach enjoy the miles and miles of empty sands. As well as being one of the most exhilarating places for riding, the firm sand and salt water are very good for the horses' legs

of their spare time attacking the ever-encroaching undergrowth on their local paths. If paths are not ridden on frequently they either become so overgrown that they tend to disappear in a mass of tangled brambles and branches, or, they can be re-graded as footpaths and horses are banned from using them. Once this happens, it is virtually impossible to have the paths reclassified. So as well as being a healthy and extremely rewarding exercise (there is something very satisfying about slashing one's way through the undergrowth) clearing a bridle-path can only add to your enjoyment of riding.

If you are lucky enough to live near the coast, riding on the empty sands can be an exhilarating experience. Miles and miles of sand, occasionally splashing through the shallows, perhaps jumping the breakwaters en route, can provide a wonderful sensation of being totally free. The horses enjoy it too, as the hard sand is an ideal surface for riding and sea water is beneficial to the horses' legs. Many trekking centres are situated within reach of beaches and much of the holiday programme will consist of long hacks over the sands.

The best advice that can be offered to any rider who wants to improve his standard and get maximum enjoyment from his time spent in the saddle, is to join his local riding club or pony club depending on the age of the rider. The Pony Club movement, which extends throughout the world has been rightly described as one of the world's great youth organisations. Begun in 1929

in Great Britain, it has grown to a membership of well over 30,000 in the British Isles and another 50,000 in other countries. A flourishing branch system enables any child who is interested in riding to join the local branch, whether they have their own pony or not. The age limit for the Pony Club is 21 and at 17 members become associates and become eligible to join the adult national movement, the Riding Club. The headquarters of both these organizations are at the National Equestrian Centre at Stoneleigh in Warwickshire while the United States has Pony Club headquarters at Pleasant Street, Dover, Massachusetts, 02030.

The object of these two organizations is to improve the standard of riding at all levels, to encourage young people to ride and to learn to enjoy all kinds of sport connected with horses and riding; to provide instruction in riding and horsemastership and to instil into people the proper care of their animals; to promote the highest ideals of sportsmanship, citizenship and loyalty thereby cultivating strength of character and self-discipline. The objects of the Riding Clubs are much the same: to assist and encourage those interested in the horse and equitation to improve and maintain the standard of riding and horsemanship and to seek to preserve and develop public riding facilities.

As well as the national qualifications that can be gained through the examination system; riding clubs and pony clubs members can take proficiency tests suitable to their own particular standard. For instance the Pony Club has efficiency tests starting with 'D'

standard and progressing to the very advanced 'A' test. Riding Clubs grade their tests from I to IV with IV requiring a very high standard. This rarely comes within the scope of the true 'weekend' rider, mainly because they do not often have the time or opportunity to ride many different horses which is one of the requirements of this standard. However, none of the tests are awarded lightly and to achieve the standards required is a commendable effort and gives the rider something to work towards.

Tests are held on set dates arranged by the club as all but the simplest require outside qualified examiners. The candidate will be examined both on his riding skill and on his practical ability involved in keeping a horse. It is by these tests that standards improve throughout the equestrian world and they give individuals a goal to work towards and a yardstick by which to measure their progress over a period of time. They are not as nerve-wracking as some people would have you believe; the examiners are highly skilled people and will know exactly how to draw the best out of a candidate to obtain the necessary results. A little dose of competition now and then is never a bad thing as it keeps people on their toes and prevents them from becoming slapdash in their outlook.

From this it will be seen that really no rider should be without membership of one or other of these clubs. They provide a wide range of competitions and activities from club level right through to the national championships and even international rallies.

The backbone of the Pony Club movement is the working rally. Members attend at a given time and place for instruction that is given by a qualified teacher. Pony Club members pay a basic subscription to their branches and then receive free instruction at rallies, both mounted and dismounted. Occasionally a small charge is made if the branch employs the services of a very highly qualified instructor or if the rally is held in a commercially run indoor school. However, such is the reputation of the Pony Club that many facilities are readily made available to branches for

little or no cost. Britain's success in international events can be traced clearly back to the work of the Pony Club. Indeed the whole of the gold medal winning team in the three-day event at Munich in 1972 had started their riding careers under the auspices of the Pony Club. And the tradition has spread all over the world.

Among the opportunities offered to members, the highlight for many members is the week spent each year at pony club camp. A full week of caring for their own pony, riding, grooming, feeding and all the associated chores do more good for a rider than months of one-hour-a-week lessons. For many children, who maybe hire their ponies, it is the one opportunity they have of caring for them to the exclusion of all else. Many branches still have their camps under canvas, which is an added attraction for many children. Although supervision has to be strict, no child seems to come away from camp with anything but a feeling of complete happiness and a little regret at the shortness of the week. Most branches find themselves fully booked each year and it also provides an opportunity for children from all backgrounds to mix together on equal terms, which is never a bad thing. Pony Club camp should not be confused with the previously mentioned summer camps in the States—these are quite different. Riding clubs too, have followed the idea and so far two or three camps have been run mainly for members of urban clubs who have little chance to care for a horse and to ride for such long periods in the open country.

Details of these camps will be found by contacting the local clubs, most of them have their own newsletters. A quick glance through the Chronicle of the Horse (the American horsey paper) will give information about the summer camps as these camps tend to advertise their facilities well before the holiday season gets going. These facilities include instruction in all forms of riding, competitions, trail riding (Western and English), stable management, as well as other sports such as golf and tennis and many establishments provide evening entertainment too.

Pony Club member taking part in the cross country phase of a pony-club event. Not all members will reach this standard but the Pony Club caters for all riders under 21

Riding Club and Pony Club competitions

If you choose to join a local club, and you would be well advised to do this as these organizations not only offer wonderful opportunities to improve your standard of horsemanship, but also provide a meeting place for people of like interest. You will find that each club will vary in its programme, but basically the fixtures arranged will consist of mounted instruction which may be given by the more experienced members of the club or by outside instructors. This form of teaching can be extremely beneficial, especially to the beginner. The lessons will often take place in a private field and some older beginners tend to feel much more relaxed in an atmosphere where they know their fellow pupils and they are not quite so overawed by the surroundings as they might be at a large commercial establishment. As well as mounted instruction, the club will probably arrange for dismounted meetings, usually during the winter months when evening instruction out of doors is not possible. These lectures can take many forms: stable management, films showing veterinary work, talks by well-known equestrian personalities, veterinary surgeons and farriers (blacksmiths), as well as visits to studs, hunt kennels, inter-club quiz evenings and many other social events.

Another advantage of belonging to a club is that they organize their own closed shows and competitions and these are especially

A more light-hearted club competition
—mounted games or gymkhana events.
Most children and their ponies enjoy
this less formal equestrian activity

suitable to the 'weekend' rider, who may find himself a little out-classed at some of the open shows in his area. Confined to members of the club, the shows are friendly affairs and essentially great fun for all taking part. It can be tremendously encouraging to ride in this type of show at the beginning of your riding career and perhaps win or be placed in one or two classes. It will give confidence to anyone who is hoping to go on and compete in bigger competitions and is often an ideal opportunity for introducing a young, inexperienced horse to the competitive scene.

Gymkhana events, or mounted games as they are often termed, are very enjoyable as they provide the chance for almost any grade of rider to take part. They should be run strictly on a relaxed basis because as soon as they become too cut-throat and competitive, they lose their essential feature, that of being strictly 'fun' classes that are enjoyed by horse and rider alike.

There are many different varieties of gymkhana events, some are more popular than others. The old favourites such as bending (a sort of horse slalom race in and out of a line of poles) are nearly always included in the schedule. A similar competition that is very popular in North America is barrel racing which is often part of the rodeo programme. Egg and spoon races, musical chairs, sacks or poles are self-explanatory, but many others such as bucket elimination where horses jump over an ever-decreasing row of buckets or cans, or potato picking scramble need a little prior explanation if the rider is to be clear about the objects of the game. Gymkhanas are relatively simple to run as the equipment needed can easily be made by members of the club. It is often a good idea, especially with young riders, to finish off a period of instruction with a few light-hearted gymkhana events or perhaps some jumping if the rally has consisted of working on the flat.

Progressing on to slightly more serious competitions, clubs

A diagram showing the type of dressage arena normally used in the less-advanced competitions. The movements are laid down on a sheet of paper and must be learnt by the rider

will organize dressage and combined events. As the word 'dressage' becomes less terrifying to the non-professional rider, so more people are keen to try their skill at producing a passable dressage test in the arena. Different tests will be used depending on the standard that the club is expecting in the entries. Before considering taking part in a dressage competition there are a few basic points to be observed. First, check on the type of test that is being used and if you feel your horse is capable of the movements required then go ahead and learn the test by heart before trying to actually ride it through. A simple test will consist of work at all three paces, walk, trot and canter on both reins. This means riding in both a left- and right-handed direction to show that the horse is both supple and obedient to the aids given by the rider. You will also have to halt at a given point in the test. All this sounds fairly simple, and in fact it is.

Someone once told me that when stripped down to the bare facts, dressage consists of doing the right thing at the right time. Obviously there is more to a test than this, but if you set out to achieve this basic fact, you will be well on the way to performing a good test. A dressage arena is a rectangular area usually 40 by 20 metres and it is marked around the sides with letters. The test will describe a series of linked movements that have to be performed within the prescribed area and at the right letters. So basically you are required to ride your horse inside the arena, changing pace and direction as set down in the test. Each movement is marked by a qualified judge who is positioned at one end

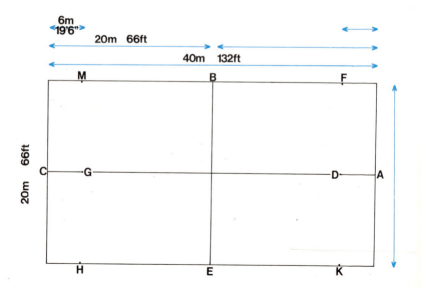

of the arena watching each horse. Marks are then totalled for the whole test and the winner will be the competitor with the highest number of good marks. Much can be learnt from riding in these tests as the judge will usually comment on each movement on the test sheet and offer advice on the performance of both horse and rider. Although it can often be discouraging to begin with, hard work and perseverance will bring results. It obviously helps to have a horse that is a good mover and naturally well balanced, but some less eye-catching animals can easily produce good tests if they are obedient to the rider's aids and calm in their appearance.

Another type of test is judged on the style of the rider and is designed to cater for those who do not perhaps get the chance to school their own horses, or maybe ride hired horses. The test is again ridden within an arena with changes of pace and direction but the judge is (or should be) looking at the rider and marking the style and position rather than the way the horse is performing.

Combined events are a stepping stone towards a full three phase event which consists of dressage, cross-country and show jumping. In combined training you will be required to perform a dressage test and then jump a round over fences on the same horse. Your two scores will then be added together to obtain a result. This competition shows the versatility of horse and rider and encourages a variety of work when training your horse.

As you become more ambitious you will probably want to compete in bigger shows with larger entries and in order to find out where these are being held you will have to obtain a calendar of events. These will be available from a variety of sources. Your local club may well know what is going on in the area. If not, one of the national magazines will carry advertisements for forthcoming shows or you can write to the appropriate national organization. For instance if you are interested in show jumping you should consult the British Show Jumping Association or the American Horse Showing Association. The best plan is to write to individual show secretaries asking for their schedule of events and then you can see if there is anything suitable for you and your horse. By mixing with other people who ride you will also get to know what is going on in your area.

Horse shows can be a good place to assess your own progress against other competitors and will give you some idea of how you are faring. Of course, not everybody will want to become involved with competitions. Many people who take up riding are quite content to ride around the countryside and obtain the maximum pleasure from this. But as with all sports, others find it stimulating and challenging to aim at a certain competition and work towards it. Whether you win or lose does not really matter, although it is obviously gratifying to go home with a ribbon or rosette for a particular class. The whole point is that you have made an extra effort to turn your horse and yourself out to a high standard and both he and you will perform to the best of your ability. Often you will find yourself producing a performance of a far higher standard than you have previously achieved, and this will be ample reward and satisfaction for your efforts.

A word of warning—don't try to compete in too many classes, both you and your horse will soon become tired and instead of enjoying the day you will find it becomes a bore and you won't want to repeat the experience. Too many people become far too serious-minded; shows should be fun but judging by the expressions to be seen on some competitors' faces (and on their horses' faces for that matter) the whole business has become far too serious and is a great strain. After all riding is meant to be a leisure activity and if you become too involved and serious minded about winning, you will soon lose the essential feeling of relaxation and enjoyment.

If you intend to compete at shows, your riding clothes may need a little supplementing. Jeans and other casual riding trousers are not smart enough. You will have to wear a well-cut pair of breeches or jodhpurs in a cream, white or fawn colour. Add to this a riding jacket which can either be made of a tweed mixture or in black, navy or a dark coloured material. Some small shows will permit you to ride in shirt sleeves if the weather is unbearably hot, but a lot of riders do not realize that jackets are not only worn for the sake of appearance. If you have a fall a jacket will offer more protection to your arms than a thin shirt. You can often sustain very nasty grazes and cuts on your arms if you skid along the hard ground after parting company with your horse. So when the show committee insists on you wearing your jacket, it is not simply because they want you to look nice. A collar and tie look neat and tidy although there is a fashion for wearing polo necked sweaters and cravats. If you want to go to great expense you can purchase a complete outfit of hunting-type clothes complete with white stock (a white hunting tie that is fixed with a mysterious knot round the neck), but for a small local show this will not be necessary, and anyway you will look rather overdressed if you arrive in clothes suited to some of the bigger, more important shows.

For Western riding there is a completely different set of clothes. What is known as a frontier suit consists of a tailored jacket with straight frontier pants to match, western boots and hat, a western shirt with a string tie or Reno-type rolled silk scarf. For casual Western riding the main difference lies in the jacket. Men will wear a stockman's coat while women will sport a suede or leather jacket or waistcoat. Obviously, as with English style riding, you can wear any clothes that you find are comfortable for Western riding provided you are not competing in a show. The saddlery of your horse in Western classes will also be quite different to the

English style. The modern Western saddle has been built with a flat seat as it has become obvious that Western riding is now followed more by those who are riding for pleasure rather than as a part of their everyday work. Some of the Western saddles are exquisitely decorated and carved and these are obviously expensive to buy. Western riding has a small following in the United Kingdom with some shows catering for the Western enthusiast. In North America it is a very different picture with whole shows and associations devoted to the promotion and continuance of Western riding.

Most competitions and shows take place during the summer months although, as the show season extends with indoor shows being held through the winter, there is a situation developing where it will soon be an all-year-round occupation. However, for the one-horse owner or weekend rider the season will be mainly a summer one. The winter has hunting to offer for those who want to take part in one of the most exciting sports of all.

Hunting
Hunting brings many emotions to the surface and I do not intend to go into the various arguments for and against hunting. It is sufficient to lay out the facts and leave each individual to decide for themselves whether they want to hunt or not.

There can be little doubt that hunting is one of the most exciting and exhilarating forms of activity open to the competent rider. The sheer thrill of riding 'blind' across country over an uncharted course has to be experienced to be appreciated. But hunting can also be an expensive form of sport. As in any club, membership fees are high. A hunt is an expensive business to run, but in return for your fees you will be able to take part in one of the oldest forms of sport known to man.

If you wish to hunt, the correct procedure is to find out the local secretary's name and approach him with a view to becoming a member of the hunt. It is extremely bad manners simply to turn up at the meet and expect to join the hunt there and then. You would not walk straight on to a golf course and expect to start playing without the usual introductions and formalities. A hunt has the same system and they are usually very pleased to see new supporters, especially young people for it is with them that the future of hunting lies.

There are many rules regarding hunt etiquette, most of which are common sense. One of the most important things to remember is that a hunt can only exist because of the good will and generosity of landowners and farmers. Without their co-operation in allowing the hunt over their land there would be no hunting at all. As you gallop over the fields, remember that you are on someone else's property and take care not to do any more damage than you can possibly help. If you are new to the hunting field, try to pick up all

the knowledge you can from the more experienced hunting folk.
Your day will be made much more interesting if you know what is
going on. Hunting, contrary to some people's views, is not one
mad gallop across country. It also involves standing around for
varying periods while hounds are working, but not necessarily
running. Ask advice about what to wear before arriving at your
first meet. A lot will depend on your own particular hunt, for
instance if you arrive dressed in the most formal attire available,
you may look completely out of place if the hunt is mainly composed of local farmers. The flowing side-saddle habits for women
are now only usually seen with some of the bigger hunts in the
more fashionable areas in the Midlands. As for shows, the main
essential is that both you and your horse look neat and tidy.
Nobody will mind how old your clothes are as long as they begin
the day clean. The chances are that at the end of a day's hunting
you will be covered with mud and some of your clothes may have
been torn by branches, but nobody minds at the end of the day as
everybody will be in much the same state.

There are various different forms of hunting—the most widely
followed is foxhunting, but drag-hunting where the hounds follow
a laid scent that has been put down by human hand, is also popular
in areas where hunting is difficult for one reason or another such
as too many main roads; motorways; too much intensive farming
or maybe not enough foxes to hunt. Drag-hunting lacks some of
the excitement of genuine hunting because the line followed is
entirely predictable whereas hunting a live quarry has an
uncertainty about it that adds to the thrill involved.

To enable you to enjoy hunting your horse should be well-
mannered in company with others, capable of jumping natural
fences and ditches and willing to stand still when required if the
hounds check during the hunt. Your horse will need to be fairly
fit if you want to follow hounds regularly and stay out for any
length of time. However it is not necessary to pay vast sums of
money for a hunter as most all-round horses will find hunting well
within their ability. The excitement of hunting seems to give most
horses an extra dose of high spirits and courage and many will
perform better in the hunting field than on an ordinary ride.

If you intend to hunt regularly there will be several tasks that
you will have to undertake before and after each hunting day. At
the approach of the winter months your horse will begin to grow
a thicker coat and if you want to hunt fairly frequently, you will
need to remove some or all of this. Clipping a horse is a job for an
expert so do not attempt to clip him yourself until you have had
some practice while watching someone else do most of the job.
If you try to do it yourself, the chances are that you will end up
with a very moth-eaten looking horse. If you intend keeping your
horse out of doors during the winter, you will only be able to take
off a little of his coat, but even this will make a considerable

difference to his comfort when he gets hot.

A trace clip will be ideal provided you compensate for the lack of hair with the specially designed rug known as a New Zealand rug. Trace clipping removes the coat from the belly, under the neck and about half way up the flanks of the horse, or 'trace-high'. The coat is left on the horse's back so that he has some protection against the cold as well as his rug. A full clip will mean that your horse will have to be kept in his stable during most of the winter months when you are not using him and this can mean a tremendous amount of work. In any case, unless you intend to hunt your horse really hard, you should not need to clip your horse right out.

Your horse will need added care and feeding before and after a day's hunting. A long day will call for a good feed the night before and a warm bed, hot mash and warm rugs after the hunting. The following day should see your horse resting with perhaps a short led walk if he is stabled, to remove any stiffness. Put yourself in your horse's place and imagine that you have spent a whole day running across country. Then you will have some idea of how your horse is feeling the day after hunting. Never forget to put your horse first when it comes to priorities. You may be desperate to sink into your hot bath, but you owe it to your horse to make him comfortable first. If he comes back from hunting hot and sweating, you must make sure that he is thoroughly dry before leaving him for the night. He must not be allowed to drink large quantities of cold water, so have some ready with the chill taken off. Look him over for any cuts or wounds that he may have sustained and if these look at all serious do not fail to call in your vet. Your horse has provided you with a day of immense fun and pleasure, the least you can do in return is to make quite sure that he is comfortable after a long, hard day.

7 INTERNATIONAL ORGANIZATIONS

Most countries today have a national organization that helps look after the interests of all riders from the top show-jumpers to the ordinary weekender. The only way to gain all the benefits of these organizations is to become a member of the relevant section of the society. For instance, in the United Kingdom, the British Horse Society (the BHS) caters for all branches of equitation except show jumping. Show jumping is covered by the British Show Jumping Association (BSJA), and racing comes under the jurisdiction of the Jockey Club.

By joining either the BHS or the BSJA, or both, riders are helping to further the work of the national organization which has its headquarters at the National Equestrian Centre at Stoneleigh in Warwickshire. Here also are the administrative offices for the Pony Club, the Riding Clubs, Dressage, Combined Training, Examinations, Riding Establishments Act Committee and other associated committees. Many people often ask the question 'Why should I join the BHS?' There are several good reasons. The BHS is the national body recognized by the government and the stronger the Society, the greater the influence with all government authorities. You also get automatic third party insurance free if you are a member. Instructional courses are arranged for members, there is much helpful literature available from HQ, and advice can always be sought from either HQ or from your local BHS representative.

The BHS guards the interests of horses and riders and helps develop riding for recreation and sport. It also aims to improve the welfare of horses and ponies and promote the interests of horse and pony breeding. It is the parent body of the Pony Club and affiliated riding clubs and runs national competitions for these organizations.

The National Equestrian Centre at Stoneleigh consists of a block of offices and the Centre itself which focuses on the mag-

nificent indoor school where many activities take place. There is a lecture room, library, seating for 300 people, and the Whitbread room which can seat over 100 people for a conference or can be used as a lounge with bar. There are also outdoor facilities including an all-weather manège, show-jumping arena and a dressage arena.

There is a cross-country course on some nearby land and a new stable yard is being constructed. The objects of the Centre are to disseminate and improve knowledge concerning horses, their management, training and use. The prime objective is to improve the standard of riding and horsemanship throughout the country. Priority is given to training instructors and the National Instructor and his assistant are both based at Stoneleigh. Courses of lessons can be taken by individuals or groups at the Centre. The National Instructor travels the country taking courses at suitable centres.

One of the most important aspects of the BHS is its work to try and provide enough qualified instructors to meet the huge demand throughout the country. The BHS operates a scheme for approving good riding schools, provides a nation-wide system of recognized professional qualifications and examinations, gives guidance and publishes information about careers with horses and advises on where to ride. British instructors are always in demand both at home and abroad and large numbers of overseas students come to the United Kingdom to gain the qualifications afforded by the BHS Examinations Committee. This surely is ample proof that Britain provides the best qualifications available.

One of the most important committees as far as the leisure rider is concerned is the Riding Establishments Committee whose objects are to assist local authorities in the efficent implementation of the Riding Establishments Act. They consider and investigate complaints in regard to licensed or unlicensed establishments. The British Horse Society issues a booklet *Where to Ride* and all the schools listed have been approved to a certain standard and have all been visited by one of the Society's qualified instructors. A similar publication *Partial List of Horse Training and Horsemanship Schools*, is issued by the US Department of Agriculture, Office of Information, Washington DC, 20250 and intending beginners would do well to obtain copies of the relevant booklet before looking for a suitable place to learn.

Although the United States has no direct equivalent to the National Equestrian Centre in Britain, there is the United States Equestrian Team Centre at Gladstone in New Jersey. Situated at Hamilton Farms it serves a rather different purpose from that of the NEC. Gladstone is really the base where the US Equestrian Teams are trained and they are extremely fortunate in that Hamilton Farms has every imaginable facility and is almost palatial in its buildings and structures. But Gladstone does not

The United States Equestrian Team trainer, Bertalan de Nemethy, offering advice to a pupil at Gladstone, New Jersey, the team training centre for the United States

Right: One of the indoor schools in use at the Potomac Horse Center, USA. This is a private enterprise that has been established to try and improve the standard of teaching and training instructors in the USA

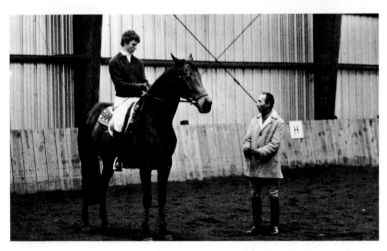

really cater for the everyday rider; it does not set out to do this. It is at Gladstone that the architect of the American show jumping team, Hungarian-born Bertalan de Nemethy, is based. So the USET deals in the main with prospective team members and possible international horses. It also includes intensive training courses for some of the outstanding Pony Club members; holders of the 'A' test, these young riders are chosen after intensive competition to train on at Gladstone. But this is only for the chosen few and America relies mainly on its individual privately run riding centres for most of its training work and provision for instructors. Occasionally, clinics or short conferences are held at Gladstone, and visitors from different states come to watch and listen to experts lecturing and demonstrating on their particular subject. Gladstone has also at times been the centre for the national three-day trials as well as dressage championships. But basically the USET is concerned with providing top-class international teams who compete with enormous success at shows and events all over the world.

In an effort to provide a centre of horsemanship education, the Potomac Horse Center was started by Mr F. G. Harting. The Center is located in the heart of the Potomac Hunt country, eighteen miles north-west of Washington D.C. and boasts some of the finest facilities to be seen at any equestrian centre in the world. There is a staff of highly qualified instructors, and many of them gained their qualifications in the United Kingdom before beginning their professional careers as instructors.

The aim of Potomac is to upgrade the standards of riding and the courses offered cover a wide range of activities including the young horse, cross-country work, stable management and all the other associated branches of equitation. Although the purpose of

such a centre is to train the prospective instructor or someone who is interested in furthering their career with horses, it has an important role to play in the encouragement of riding as a leisure occupation. It is only by providing more instructors that the overall standard among all riders can improve.

Other countries too have their training centres but many are run on a purely commercial basis with money-making shows and events being held while the important aspect of tuition, and training instructors is often neglected. There is nothing wrong with this, there will always be a demand for new shows and events but it is in the interests of the whole riding public that the more workaday side of the picture should not take a minor place in the equestrian world.

The governing body of the world equestrian scene, with the exception of racing, is the *Federation Equestre International* or FEI as it is known, which has its headquarters in Brussels. All official international events are run under FEI rules and the Federation acts as the international liaison body on all matters of policy. It is unlikely that the weekend rider will have any contact with this organization, but it is useful to know who has the final word in any dispute arising in the international riding world.

The American Horse Shows Association is basically concerned with the running of the larger shows, helping to organize courses and acting as an advisory body, but they do not function on quite the same lines as the BHS. It would be invidious to mention some establishments by name and leave out others that do equally fine work in the production of qualified staff, and in teaching the beginner. The best plan is to consult the national organization and ask their advice on the suitability of each place. If you want to go on an intensive course of a full week of lessons, you only find out by taking into consideration the reputation of each establishment.

The FEI's chairman is HRH Prince Philip and his influence in the equestrian world is well known. He is not simply a figurehead, he takes a keen and active interest in all forms of riding and takes his position as chairman of the governing body very seriously.

The interest shown and the active part taken by various members of the British Royal Family has done much to increase the interest in horses and riding, not only in the UK but all over the world. How can the layman fail to become interested when almost every day one or other of the English national newspapers mentions equestrian activities of the Royal Family. The Queen is an acknowledged expert in the racing world and clearly some of her happiest moments are spent on the racecourse or on the early morning gallops watching her horses in training. Her mother has a stable of top-class steeplechasers while her daughter, Princess Anne, is champion of Europe in the three day event. The Prince of Wales is a keen and talented polo player.

Certainly this Royal patronage has encouraged more people to take an interest in riding and also it has provided a new form of spectator-sport. Because of the participation of well-known figures in competitive events, the man in the street has become an interested spectator in a sport that was originally thought of as purely an activity for the wealthy. Maybe the high-powered competitive scene is still too costly for the ordinary rider to consider, but he can still take his enjoyment from his everyday riding and it is in this sphere that there has been such a surge of interest.

Although not strictly under the heading of leisure riding, we must not forget the fantastic work done in the sphere of teaching riding to disabled and severely handicapped people, both adults and children. Riding for the disabled has taken an enormous leap forward over the past few years. For many of these less fortunate people, horses have opened up a whole new world. In the British Isles the national organizing body is the Riding for the Disabled Association which has its headquarters at the NEC at Stoneleigh.

When a handicapped person is able to ride, usually with the assistance of several willing helpers on the ground, a new dimension is added to their life. Many are so severely handicapped that their only method of movement is by constant assistance from others. The moment they are put on the very quiet horses and ponies that are used, they are provided with a new method of movement. The pony's legs substitute for their own and they are at last mobile. The unparalleled sense of unaccustomed freedom and achievement has been shown to be one of the best remedies available to the disabled. Not only physically but mentally handicapped children and adults are provided with the chance to learn to ride. The enjoyment and sheer pleasure on the faces of these riders has to be seen to be truly appreciated.

Helping disabled persons in this way can also offer wonderful

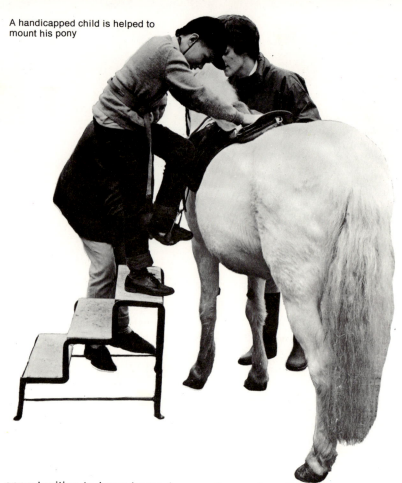

A handicapped child is helped to mount his pony

opportunities to keen horse-lovers who are happily able to ride and walk without assistance. The local groups of the RDA need an endless supply of willing helpers to lead the ponies and, in many cases, to assist some of the riders in their efforts to ride. This then can be another way of enjoying horses and at the same time of being of inestimable value to a wonderful association. It might at first sight appear to be something of a chore, but I can only say that to help further riding in this way can be one of the most satisfying sides of contact with horses. Riding not only assists on the psychological side with the patients, it can also serve as a remedial exercise to help improve the physical health of the handicapped. Riding employs muscles that otherwise might not come into use and, like swimming, riding is often prescribed to help a handicapped person. Local associations are always anxious to obtain more helpers, so if you want to come into contact with horses and ponies and also help a good cause, this could be the answer. It may not be quite as personally exciting as actually riding for yourself, but it has a lot to offer if you want to combine helping others with a love of horses.

GLOSSARY

Action The manner in which a horse moves, good, bad or indifferent

Aged A horse more than eight years old

Aids The communications from rider to horse conveying the wishes of the rider. These can be natural: hands, legs, seat, voice and weight of body or artificial: whip, spurs and various articles of tack such as martingales and specialized nosebands

Anglo-Arab Offspring of thoroughbred-Arab cross

Appaloosa Spotted horse or pony, originally the mount of the Nez Perce Indians

Bay Colour of a horse. This varies from a medium brown to dark brown, with black mane and tail and black points

Bedding Material used in the stable to enable the horse to lie down comfortably. May be straw, shavings, sawdust, peat moss etc

Blaze A white facial mark running the length of the horse's face

Blemish Unsightly scar or mark left from an injury to the horse's body. A horse with such a scar will rarely win in the show ring

Blood Horse Thoroughbred type

Bolt A very serious vice in any horse as he runs away uncontrollably. Also used to describe a horse that gobbles its feed

Bridle The harness that fits over the horse's head, which with a bit in the horse's mouth makes control possible

Box To lead a horse into a trailer or horse box. A horse may be described as 'good to box' or the opposite.

Bran Mash Feed of bran mixed with boiling water and left to cool before being administered. Very useful for sick horses and as a laxative

Break To break a horse in in the process by which the human proceeds to train and school a horse

Broken-wind A serious respiratory fault caused usually by working an unfit horse too hard and fast, or after excessive feeding. Incurable

Cannon bone The shin bone of a horse

Canter Three time pace of the horse that precedes the fastest pace of all, the gallop

Cap Fee paid by a guest who joins a hunt on one or two occasions. Members do not normally have to pay a capping fee

Chestnut Colour of horse, similar to bronze or copper but can vary from very pale to a deep reddish tinge. Often known in the United States as 'sorrel'. Alternatively a chestnut is the horny little growth present on the inside of a horse's legs

Cinch The girth of a Western saddle

Cold-blooded Usually a large, heavy-boned and coarse type of horse, originating from north-west Europe and northern Asia

Colic Painful and sometimes fatal stomach ache in the horse

Collect A manner of going where a horse is perfectly balanced, with his hindquarters well under him, his head in the correct position and so he is ready to carry out any movement required by his rider

Combination horse Used for both riding and driving

Condition A horse 'in condition' is in good health, fit and ready to work hard, coat glossy, eyes bright and sound in all respects

Conformation The physique and general make-up of a horse. Show classes are judged partly on conformation and this is referred to as good or bad, depending on the make and shape of the horse before the judge

Cooling off Drying a horse off and generally relaxing him after a particularly strenuous effort

Corn A bruise on the sole of the foot that will cause the horse a great deal of pain and render him useless for work until it has recovered

Cutting horse A western term for a horse that has been trained to sort cattle and cut them out individually from a herd

Dam The mother of a horse

Dapple-grey Grey horse with darker spots on the coat

Dun Fawn or beige coloured coated horse with blackish mane and tail and an eel strip down the middle of the back

Farrier Blacksmith

Forage All horse food

Filled legs Swollen legs, caused for a variety of reasons, too little work, too much hard work on an unfit horse, direct injury or overfeeding

Filly Female horse under four years

Forehand The front part of the horse including head, neck, shoulders and front legs

Forelock Part of the mane that extends between the horse's ears

Fresh Used to describe a horse when it is excitable perhaps because it is short of exercise or overfed

Frog Part of the horse's foot

Gaited Refers to American saddlebreds. They are either three gaited or five gaited, the word gait meaning pace

Gallop The fastest pace of a horse

Gelding A castrated male horse

Girth Band of various materials, leather, nylon, webbing etc that passes under the horse's belly to attach the saddle to his back

Green horse Unschooled and uneducated horse

Graze To feed on grass in a meadow

Hack Riding horse or the term used to describe trail or pleasure riding i.e. 'to go for a hack'

Halter Rope or leather head harness used to tie horse up during grooming, shoeing etc

Hand Unit for measuring a horse, 4 inches

Hindquarters The part of the body from behind the barrel of the horse.

Jog Very slow trot, required in Western classes, but looked upon in other cases as a bad manner of moving

Keep Used to refer to grazing available for horses, i.e. 'good keep' would be a good meadow of grass and 'poor keep' a run-down and badly kept field offering little in the way of nutrition to a horse

Leading leg The foreleg that leads in the canter movement

Leathers Usually refers to the strap that supports the stirrup iron and is attached to the saddle on the stirrup bar

Livery stable A stable that keeps horses for owners at an agreed fee per week, in return for looking after and exercizing the horse

Lope A contraction of the word 'gallop', this term is used to describe the canter in Western riding

Loose Box or 'Box' A horse's stable, where the horse can move at will, lie down etc. Different from a stall where the horse is secured by the head to a fitting and does not have so much freedom

Lunge The exercise whereby the trainer has control of the horse from the ground by means of a long rein attached to a specially designed cavesson (a special padded type of noseband). The horse circles the trainer at different paces. Often used when instructing beginners on a quiet, well-trained horse

Manger Container in the stable for horse fodder

Mane Long hair growing from the crest of the horse

Mash See bran mash

Mount The action of getting up on a horse by placing the left foot in the stirrup and springing up into the saddle. Dismounting is effected on the same side of the horse, that is the near side or left hand side of the horse, when viewed from behind

Muck out The action of cleaning out a horse's stable after he has been kept in for any time

Near side See under 'mount'

Nappy Term used to describe a stubborn horse that refuses to obey the rider's aids

Nose band Strap that goes round the nose, part of the bridle; there are several varieties of noseband

Numnah A pad of some material, sheepskin, felt, leather or quilted cotton that goes underneath the saddle to prevent excessive pressure

Off-side The right hand side of the horse when viewed from behind

Piebald A horse of two colours, black and white in large patches

Pinto Multi-coloured horse, term used in USA

Plaited mane A mane that has been divided up into a number of small plaits, usually for showing or hunting to smarten the appearance of the horse. The tail can also be plaited, at the top, to add to the turnout

Pony A horse under the height of 14.2 hh is usually referred to as a pony

Quarter-horse A breed developed in

America, specially to race at speed over a quarter of a mile

Rack A four beat gait in which each foot comes down alone at speed in turn. This is not a natural gait for a horse and it is therefore difficult for a horse to master such a movement.

Rear A highly dangerous vice, when the horse stands on his hind legs. The danger is that he may tip over backwards

Rein back The action of making a horse take steps backwards at a given aid from the rider

A ride Apart from the obvious meaning, this can be a designated path that has been specially cleared perhaps through a woodland area

Roan Colour of a horse where the basic colour is interspersed by white hairs in the coat

Rough off to turn a horse out to grass after a strenuous period of work such as the end of the hunting season. This must be done gradually otherwise it will be too much of a shock to the horse's system

Rubber A linen cloth used for a final polish on the horse's coat

Rub down To groom a horse that has sweated up after work or is wet from being out in the rain, Rubbing down is done with straw, hay and a stable rubber

Rug up The action of putting rugs on a horse while he is in the stable

Saddle soap A special soap that is used to clean all leather work, preserve it and keep it supple for use

Salt lick A block of salt provided for a horse to lick to aid its diet

Skewbald Colour of horses composed of white and any colour except black

Sock White marking on a horse's legs that reaches a little way up the leg, further up to the knee it becomes a stocking

Skip A plastic, rubber or wicker basket for collecting manure from the stable

Slug A lazy horse that requires a great deal of encouragement to get it to move in any fashion at all

Strap Another term for grooming a horse

Tack Term used to refer to saddlery, from this follows tack room, tack cleaning etc

Trail horse A horse used exclusively for riding trails in USA, the equivalent in the UK would be a hack

Tree The frame inside a saddle on which the saddle is built. Most modern saddles have spring trees

Unsound Used to describe a horse that is either lame, or is afflicted in its health in some way and is not therefore capable of being used for riding

Withers A point of the horse from which measurement in hands is made. The withers are at the base of the crest just in front of where the saddle naturally sits

Further Reading

Books

Chamberlain, H. *Training Hunters, Jumpers and Hacks*, New York, 1972.

Hayes, M & Jacobson, P. *A Horse Around the House*, New York, 1972.

Herman, P. *The Family Horse*, New York, 1959.

Littauer, Capt. V. S. *Common Sense Horsemanship*, New York, 1963.

Pinch, D. H. *Happy Horsemanship*, New York, 1967.

The Pony Club: Keeping a Pony at Grass, London, 1958.

Manual of Horsemanship, London, 1972.

Training the Young Pony, London, 1964.

Williams, J. *Introduction to Hunting*, London, 1970, New York, 1972.

Wynmalen, H. *Dressage*, London, 1969, New York, 1954.

Equitation, New York, 1972.

Magazines

Horse and Hound (UK)
Chronicle of the Horse (USA)
Hoofs and Horns (Australia)
Rider (Australia)

There are also several useful publications issued by the US Department of Agriculture, Office of Information, Washington DC, 20250, that will assist in many ways. Some booklets are also obtainable from the University of California, Agricultural Extension Service, Davis, California, 95616.

One of the best bookshops, who are quite willing to send books to all parts of the world, are J. A. Allen, The Horseman's Bookshop, 1 Lower Grosvenor Place, London S.W.1.

INDEX